CHOCOLATE
FANTASIES

CHOCOLATE
FANTASIES

70 IRRESISTIBLE RECIPES TO DIE FOR

Christine France

SWEET WATER PRESS

First published in 1998 by Sweetwater Press
by arrangement with Anness Publishing Limited

Produced by Anness Publishing Limited
Hermes House
88–89 Blackfriars Road
London SE1 8HA

ISBN 1-58173-020-9

Publisher: Joanna Lorenz
Project Editors: Joanne Rippin, Linda Doeser
Designers: Nigel Partridge, Siân Keogh
Special Photography: Don Last

Front Cover: Lisa Tai, Designer; Thomas Odulate, Photographer;
Helen Trent, Stylist; Lucy McKelvie, Home Economist

Previously published as part of a larger compendium: *The Ultimate Encyclopedia of Chocolate*

Printed in Hong Kong/China

10 9 8 7 6 5 4 3 2 1

The authors and publishers would like to thank the following people for supplying
additional recipes in the book: Catherine Atkinson, Alex Barker, Carla Capalbo,
Maxine Clark, Frances Cleary, Carole Clements, Roz Denny, Nicola Diggins,
Joanne Farrow, Silvana Franco, Sarah Gates, Shirley Gill, Patricia Lousada,
Norma MacMillan, Sue Maggs, Sarah Maxwell, Janice Murfitt, Annie Nichols,
Angela Nilsen, Louise Pickford, Katherine Richmond, Hilaire Walden, Laura
Washburn, Steven Wheeler, Judy Williams, Elizabeth Wolf-Cohen.

Additional recipe photographs supplied by: Karl Adamson, Edward Allwright,
David Armstrong, Steve Baxter, James Duncan, Michelle Garrett, Amanda
Heywood, Tim Hill, David Jordan.

NOTE
All standard spoon and cup measures are level.

CONTENTS

INTRODUCTION

Few people can resist it—whether a sumptuous and self-indulgent chocolate cake, a plate of melt-in-the-mouth profiteroles, a richly coated sundae, or a decorative box of truffles. This book is packed with wickedly tempting recipes for those with a sweet tooth, chocolate-lovers, and self-admitted, outright "chocoholics."

The book is divided into six chapters with over 70 recipes for preparing superb confections with dark (or bittersweet), milk and white chocolate. Rich Cakes ranges from morning coffee and afternoon tea-time treats, such as Chocolate Coconut Roulade and Frosted Chocolate Fudge, to magnificent dinner party centerpieces, such as Chocolate Red Currant Torte and Meringue Cake with Chocolate Mascarpone. Hot Desserts includes such magical delights as Chocolate Crêpes with Plums and Port and Dark Chocolate Ravioli with White Chocolate and Cream Cheese Filling. Tarts, Pies & Cheesecakes boasts such favorites as Chocolate Tiramisu Tart and Mississippi Mud Pie, while Cold Desserts tantalizes the tastebuds with a selection of sorbets and ice creams. Anything from Little Cakes, Cookies & Bars will bring the children running, while Candy & Truffles offers more sophisticated pleasures, such as Double Chocolate-dipped Fruit, Rich Chocolate Pistachio Fudge, and Cognac and Ginger Creams.

There is hardly a country in the western world that does not have chocolate as part of its culinary culture, whether it be a moist chocolate brownie from the United States, a chocolate-covered pancake from Hungary, or an elegant French pastry. Indulge yourself on a chocolate-lover's dream journey—your only problem will be what to choose next!

TECHNIQUES
❧ ~ ❧

MELTING CHOCOLATE

If chocolate is being melted on its own, all the equipment must be completely dry, as water may cause the chocolate to thicken and become a stiff paste. For this reason, do not cover chocolate during or after melting it, as condensation could form. If chocolate does thicken, add a little shortening (not butter or margarine) and mix well. If this does not work, start again. Do not discard the thickened chocolate; melt it with cream to make a sauce.

With or without liquid, chocolate should be melted very slowly. It is easily burned or scorched, and then develops a bad flavor. If any steam gets into the chocolate, it can turn into a solid mass. If this happens, stir in a little shortening. Dark chocolate should not be heated above 120°F. Milk and white chocolate should not be heated above 110°F. Take particular care when melting white chocolate, which curdles very easily when subjected to heat.

MELTING CHOCOLATE OVER SIMMERING WATER

<u>1</u> Chop or cut chocolate into small pieces with a sharp knife so it will melt quickly and evenly.

<u>2</u> Put the chocolate in the top of a double boiler or in a heatproof bowl over a saucepan of barely simmering water. The bowl should not touch the water.

<u>3</u> Heat gently until the chocolate is melted and smooth, stirring occasionally. Remove from the heat and stir.

MELTING CHOCOLATE OVER DIRECT HEAT

When a recipe recommends melting chocolate with a liquid such as milk, cream or even butter, this can be done over direct heat in a saucepan.

<u>1</u> Choose a heavy saucepan. Add the chocolate and liquid and melt over low heat, stirring frequently, until the chocolate is melted and the mixture is smooth. Remove from heat immediately. This method is also used for making sauces, icings and some candies.

<u>2</u> Chocolate can also be melted in a very low oven. Preheat oven to 225°F. Put the chocolate in an ovenproof bowl and place in the oven for a few minutes. Remove the chocolate before it is completely melted and stir until smooth.

MELTING CHOCOLATE IN THE MICROWAVE

Check the chocolate at frequent intervals during the cooking time. These times are for a 650–700 W oven and are approximate, as microwave ovens vary.

<u>1</u> Place 4 ounces chopped or broken dark, bittersweet or semi-sweet chocolate in a microwave-safe bowl and microwave on Medium for about 2 minutes. The same quantity of milk or white chocolate should be melted on Low for about 2 minutes.

<u>2</u> Check the chocolate frequently during the cooking time. The chocolate will not change shape, but will start to look shiny. It must then be removed from the microwave and stirred until completely melted and smooth.

TEMPERING CHOCOLATE

TEMPERING CHOCOLATE

Tempering is the process of gently heating and cooling chocolate to stabilize the emulsification of cocoa solids and butterfat. This technique is generally used by professionals handling couverture chocolate. It allows the chocolate to shrink quickly (to allow easy release from a mold, for example with Easter eggs) or to be kept at room temperature for several weeks or months without losing its crispness and shiny surface. All solid chocolate is tempered in production, but once melted loses its "temper" and must be tempered again unless it is to be used immediately.

Untempered chocolate tends to "bloom" or becomes dull and streaky or takes on a cloudy appearance. This can be avoided if the melted chocolate is refrigerated immediately: Chilling the chocolate solidifies the cocoa butter and prevents it from rising to the surface and "blooming." General baking and dessert-making do not require tempering, which is a relatively involved procedure and takes practice. However, it is useful to be aware of the technique when preparing sophisticated decorations, molded chocolates or coatings. Most shapes can be made without tempering if they are chilled immediately.

EQUIPMENT

To temper chocolate successfully, you will need a marble slab or similar cool, smooth surface, such as an upturned baking sheet. A flexible plastic scraper is ideal for spreading the chocolate, but you can use a metal spatula. As the temperature is crucial, you will need a chocolate thermometer. Look for this at a specialty kitchen supply shop, where you may also find blocks of tempered chocolate, ready for immediate use.

1 Break the chocolate into small pieces and place it into the top of a double boiler or a heatproof bowl over a saucepan of hot water. Heat gently until just melted.

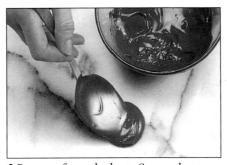

2 Remove from the heat. Spoon about three-quarters of the melted chocolate onto a marble slab or other cool, smooth, non-porous work surface.

3 With a flexible plastic scraper or metal spatula, spread the chocolate thinly, then scoop it up before spreading it again. Repeat the sequence, constantly working the chocolate for about 5 minutes.

4 Using a chocolate thermometer, check the temperature of the chocolate as you work it. As soon as the temperature registers 82°F, transfer the chocolate back into the bowl and stir into the remaining chocolate.

5 With the addition of the hot chocolate, the temperature should now be 90°F, making the chocolate ready for use. To test, drop a little of the chocolate from a spoon onto the marble; it should set very quickly.

STORING CHOCOLATE

Chocolate can be stored successfully for up to a year if the conditions are favorable. This means a dry place with a temperature of around 68°F. At higher temperatures, the chocolate may develop white streaks as the fat comes to the surface. Although this will not spoil the flavor, it will mar the appearance of the chocolate, making it unsuitable for use as a decoration. When storing chocolate, keep it cool and dry. Place inside an airtight container, away from strong smelling foods. Check the "best before" dates on the package.

Chocolate Piping

Pipe chocolate directly onto a cake, or onto baking parchment to make cutouts, small outlined shapes or irregular designs. After melting the chocolate, let it cool slightly so it just coats the back of a spoon. If it still flows freely it will be too runny to hold its shape when piped. When it is the right consistency, you then need to work fast as the chocolate will set quickly. Use a paper piping bag and keep the pressure very tight, as the chocolate will flow readily without encouragement.

Making a Paper Piping Bag

A non-stick paper cone is ideal for piping small amounts of messy liquids like chocolate as it is small, easy to handle and disposable, unlike a conventional piping bag, which will need cleaning.

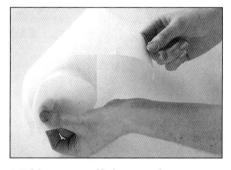

1 Fold a square of baking parchment in half to form a triangle. With the triangle point facing you, fold the left corner down to the center.

2 Fold the right corner down and wrap it around the folded left corner to form a cone. Fold the ends into the cone.

3 Spoon the melted chocolate into the cone and fold the top edges over. When ready to pipe, snip off the end of the point neatly to make a tiny hole, about ⅛ inch in diameter.

4 Another method is to use a small heavy-duty freezer or plastic bag. Place a piping nozzle in one corner of the bag, so that it is in the correct position for piping. Fill as above, squeezing the filling into one corner and twisting the top to seal. Snip off the corner of the bag, if necessary, so that the tip of the nozzle emerges, and squeeze gently to pipe the design.

Chocolate Drizzles

You can have great fun making random shapes or, with a steady hand, special designs that will look great on cakes or cookies.

1 Melt the chocolate and pour it into a paper cone or small piping bag fitted with a very small plain nozzle. Drizzle the chocolate onto a baking sheet lined with baking parchment to make small, connecting shapes, such as circles or squares. Let set for 30 minutes, then peel off the paper.

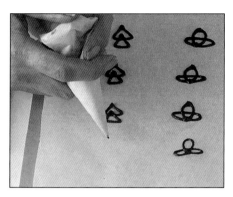

2 Chocolate can be used in many designs, such as flowers or butterflies. Use baking parchment as tracing paper and pipe the chocolate over the chosen design or decorative shape.

3 For butterflies, pipe chocolate onto individually cut squares and wait until it just begins to set. Use a long, thin box (like an egg carton) and place the butterfly shape in the box or between the cups so it is bent in the center, creating the butterfly shape. Chill until needed.

Piping onto Cakes

This looks effective on top of a cake iced with coffee glaze.

1 Melt 2 ounces each of white and plain dark chocolate in separate bowls, and let cool slightly. Place the chocolates in separate paper piping bags. Cut a small piece off the pointed end of each bag in a straight line.

2 Hold each piping bag in turn above the surface of the cake and pipe the chocolates all over as shown in the picture. Alternatively, pipe a freehand design in one continuous curvy line, first with one bag of chocolate, then the other.

PIPING CURLS

Make lots of these curly shapes and store them in a cool place ready for use as cake decorations. Try piping the lines in contrasting colors of chocolate to vary the effect.

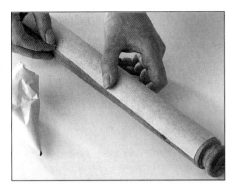

1 Melt 4 ounces chocolate and let cool slightly. Cover a rolling pin with baking parchment and attach it with tape. Fill a paper piping bag with the chocolate and cut a small piece off the pointed end in a straight line.

2 Pipe lines of chocolate backward and forward over the baking parchment.

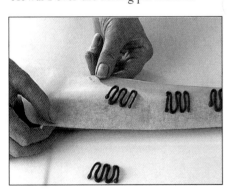

3 Let the piped curls set in a cool place, then carefully peel off the baking parchment. Use a metal spatula to lift the curls onto the cake.

FEATHERING OR MARBLING CHOCOLATE

These two related techniques provide some of the easiest and most effective ways of decorating the top of a cake, and they are also used when making a swirled mixture for cutouts. Chocolate sauce and heavy cream can also be feathered or marbled to decorate a dessert.

1 Melt two contrasting colors of chocolate and spread one over the cake or surface to be decorated.

2 Spoon the contrasting chocolate into a piping bag and pipe lines or swirls over the chocolate base.

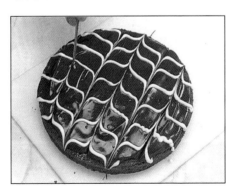

3 Working quickly before the chocolate sets, draw a skewer or toothpick through the swirls to create a feathered or marbled effect.

CHOCOLATE CUTOUTS

Try piping the outline in one color of chocolate and filling in the middle with another. The effect can be dramatic.

1 Tape a piece of wax paper to a baking sheet or flat board. Draw around a shaped cookie cutter onto the paper several times. Secure a piece of baking parchment over the top.

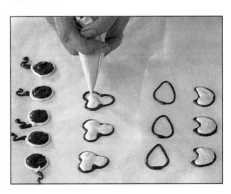

2 Pipe over the outline of your design in a continuous thread.

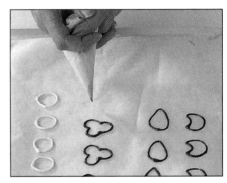

3 Cut the end off the other bag, making the hole slightly wider than before, and pipe the chocolate to fill in the outline so it looks slightly rounded. Let the shapes set in a cool place, then carefully lift them off the baking parchment with a metal spatula.

RICH CAKES

FRENCH CHOCOLATE CAKE

SERVES 10

*9 ounces bittersweet chocolate, chopped into
small pieces
1 cup unsalted butter, cut into small pieces
scant ½ cup sugar
2 tablespoons brandy or orange-flavored
liqueur
5 eggs
1 tablespoon all-purpose flour
confectioners' sugar, for dusting
whipped or sour cream, for serving*

<u>1</u> Preheat oven to 350°F. Generously
grease a 9 x 2-inch springform pan. Line
the base with baking parchment and
grease. Wrap the bottom and sides of the
pan in foil to prevent water from seeping
through into the cake.

<u>2</u> In a saucepan, over low heat, melt the
chocolate, butter and sugar, stirring
frequently until smooth. Remove from
the heat, cool slightly and stir in the
brandy or liqueur.

<u>3</u> In a large bowl beat the eggs lightly for
one minute. Beat in the flour, then slowly
beat in the chocolate mixture until well
blended. Pour into the pan.

<u>4</u> Place the springform pan in a large
roasting pan. Add enough boiling water
to come ¾ inch up the side of the
springform pan. Bake for 25–30 minutes,
until the edge of the cake is set but the
center is still soft. Remove the
springform pan from the roasting pan and
remove the foil. Cool on a wire rack. The
cake will sink in the center and become
its classic slim shape as it cools. Don't
worry if the surface cracks slightly.

<u>5</u> Remove the side of the springform pan
and turn the cake onto a wire rack. Lift
off the pan's base and then carefully peel
back the paper, so the bottom of the cake
is now the top. Leave the cake on the rack
until it is completely cool.

<u>6</u> Cut 6–8 strips of baking parchment
1 inch wide and place randomly over the
cake. Dust the cake with confectioners'
sugar, then carefully remove the paper.
Slide the cake onto a plate and serve with
whipped or sour cream.

MERINGUE CAKE WITH CHOCOLATE MASCARPONE

SERVES ABOUT 10

4 egg whites
pinch of salt
¾ cup sugar
1 teaspoon ground cinnamon
3 ounces dark chocolate, grated
confectioners' sugar and rose petals, to decorate

FOR THE FILLING

4 ounces unsweetened chocolate, chopped into
small pieces
1 teaspoon vanilla extract or rosewater
½ cup mascarpone cheese

1 Preheat oven to 300°F. Line two large baking sheets with baking parchment. Whisk the egg whites with the salt in a clean, grease-free bowl until they form stiff peaks.

2 Gradually whisk in half the sugar, then add the rest and whisk until the meringue is very stiff and glossy. Add the cinnamon and chocolate and whisk lightly to mix.

3 Draw an 8-inch circle on the lining paper on one of the baking sheets, replace it upside down and spread the marked circle evenly with about half the meringue. Spoon the remaining meringue in 28–30 small neat heaps on both baking sheets. Bake for 1½ hours, until crisp.

4 To make the filling, melt the chocolate in a heatproof bowl over hot water. Cool slightly, then add the vanilla or rosewater and the cheese. Cool the mixture until it holds its shape.

5 Spoon the chocolate mixture into a large piping bag and sandwich the meringues together in pairs, reserving a small amount of filling for assembling the cake.

6 Arrange the filled meringues on a serving platter, piling them up in a pyramid. Keep them in position with a few well-placed dabs of the reserved filling. Dust the pyramid with confectioners' sugar, sprinkle with the rose petals and serve immediately, while the meringues are crisp.

CHOCOLATE ALMOND MOUSSE CAKE

SERVES 8

*2 ounces unsweetened dark chocolate, broken
into squares*
7 ounces marzipan, grated or chopped
scant 1 cup milk
1 cup self-rising flour
2 eggs, separated
½ cup light brown sugar

FOR THE MOUSSE FILLING

*4 ounces unsweetened chocolate, chopped into
small pieces*
¼ cup unsalted butter
2 eggs, separated
2 tablespoons Amaretto di Saronno liqueur

FOR THE TOPPING

1 recipe Chocolate Ganache
toasted sliced almonds, to decorate

1 Preheat oven to 375°F. Grease a deep 6½-inch square cake pan and line with baking parchment. Combine the chocolate, marzipan and milk in a saucepan and heat gently without boiling, stirring until smooth.

2 Sift the flour into a bowl and add the chocolate mixture and egg yolks, beating until evenly mixed.

3 Whisk the egg whites in a clean, grease-free bowl until stiff enough to hold firm peaks. Whisk in the sugar gradually. Stir about 1 tablespoon of the whites into the chocolate mixture to lighten it, then fold in the rest.

4 Spoon the mixture into the pan, spreading it evenly. Bake for 45–50 minutes, until springy and firm to the touch. Let cool on a wire rack.

5 To make the mousse filling, melt the chocolate with the butter in a small saucepan over low heat, then remove from the heat and beat in the egg yolks and Amaretto. Whisk the egg whites in a clean, grease-free bowl until stiff, then fold into the chocolate mixture.

6 Slice the cold cake in half across the middle to make two even layers. Return one half to the clean cake pan and pour the chocolate mousse over it. Top with the second layer of cake and press down lightly. Chill until set.

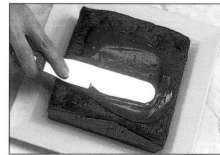

7 Turn the cake out onto a serving plate. Let the chocolate ganache soften to room temperature, then beat it to a soft, spreading consistency. Spread the chocolate ganache over the top and sides of the cake, then press the almonds over the sides. Serve chilled.

SACHERTORTE

SERVES 10–12

*8 ounces dark chocolate, chopped into
small pieces*
⅔ cup butter, softened
½ cup sugar
8 eggs, separated
1 cup all-purpose flour
FOR THE GLAZE
scant 1 cup apricot jam
1 tablespoon lemon juice
FOR THE ICING
8 ounces dark chocolate, cut into small pieces
scant 1 cup sugar
1 tablespoon corn syrup
1 cup heavy cream
1 teaspoon vanilla extract
chocolate leaves, to decorate

1 Preheat oven to 350°F. Grease a 9-inch round springform cake pan and line with baking parchment. Melt the chocolate in a heatproof bowl over barely simmering water, then set the bowl aside.

2 Cream the butter with the sugar in a mixing bowl until light and fluffy, then add the egg yolks, one at a time, beating after each addition. Beat in the melted chocolate, then sift the flour over the mixture and fold it in evenly.

3 Whisk the egg whites in a clean, grease-free bowl until stiff, then stir about a quarter of the whites into the chocolate mixture to lighten it. Fold in the remaining whites.

4 Pour the chocolate mixture into the prepared cake pan and spread evenly. Bake for about 50–55 minutes or until firm. Cool in the pan for 5 minutes, then turn out carefully onto a wire rack and let cool completely.

5 To make the glaze, heat the apricot jam with the lemon juice in a small saucepan until melted, then strain through a sieve into a bowl. Once the cake is completely cool, slice in half across the middle to make two even-size layers.

6 Brush the top and sides of each layer with the apricot glaze, then sandwich them together. Place on a wire rack.

7 To make the icing, mix the chocolate, sugar, corn syrup, cream and vanilla in a heavy saucepan. Heat gently, stirring constantly, until the mixture is thick and smooth. Simmer gently for 3–5 minutes, without stirring, until the mixture registers 200°F on a sugar thermometer. Pour the icing quickly over the cake, spreading to cover the top and sides completely. Let set, decorate with chocolate leaves, then serve with whipped cream, if desired.

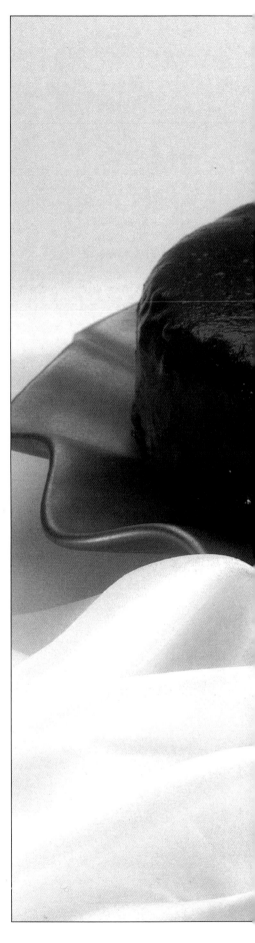

BLACK FOREST CAKE

4 Prick each layer all over with a skewer or fork, then sprinkle with Kirsch. Using a hand-held electric mixer, whip the cream in a bowl until it starts to thicken, then gradually beat in the confectioners' sugar and vanilla until the mixture begins to hold its shape.

5 To assemble, spread one cake layer with a thick layer of flavored cream and top with about half the cherries. Spread a second cake layer with cream, top with the remaining cherries, then place it on top of the first layer. Top with the final cake layer.

6 Spread the remaining cream all over the cake. Dust a plate with confectioners' sugar, and position the cake carefully in the center. Press grated chocolate over the sides and decorate the cake with the chocolate curls and fresh or drained cherries.

SERVES 8–10
6 eggs
scant 1 cup sugar
1 teaspoon vanilla extract
½ cup all-purpose flour
½ cup cocoa powder
½ cup unsalted butter, melted

FOR THE FILLING AND TOPPING
¼ cup Kirsch
2½ cups heavy cream
2 tablespoons confectioners' sugar
½ teaspoon vanilla extract
1½-pound jar pitted sour cherries, well drained

TO DECORATE
confectioners' sugar, for dusting
grated chocolate
Chocolate Curls
fresh or drained canned sour cherries

1 Preheat oven to 350°F. Grease three 7½-inch cake pans. Line the bottom of each with baking parchment. Combine the eggs with the sugar and vanilla in a bowl and beat with a hand-held electric mixer until very thick.

2 Sift the flour and cocoa powder over the mixture and fold in lightly and evenly with a metal spoon. Gently stir in the melted butter.

3 Divide the mixture among the prepared cake pans, smoothing them evenly. Bake for 15–18 minutes, until the cakes are springy and firm to the touch. Let them cool in the pans for about 5 minutes, then turn over onto wire racks and let cool completely. Remove the lining paper from each cake layer.

CHOCOLATE GINGER CRUNCH CAKE

SERVES 6

5 ounces unsweetened chocolate, chopped into small pieces
¼ cup unsalted butter
4 ounces ginger cookies
4 pieces preserved stem ginger
2 tablespoons preserved ginger syrup
3 tablespoons shredded coconut

TO DECORATE

1 ounce milk chocolate, chopped into small pieces
pieces of candied ginger

1 Grease a 6-inch flan ring and place it on a sheet of baking parchment. Melt the chocolate with the butter in a heatproof bowl over barely simmering water. Remove from the heat and set aside.

2 Crush the cookies into small pieces. Pour them into a bowl.

3 Chop fine the preserved ginger and mix with the crushed ginger cookies.

4 Stir the cookie mixture, ginger syrup and coconut into the melted chocolate and butter, mixing well until evenly combined.

5 Pour the mixture into the prepared flan ring and press down firmly and evenly. Refrigerate until set.

6 Remove the flan ring and slide the cake onto a plate. Melt the milk chocolate, drizzle it over the top and decorate with the pieces of candied ginger.

FROSTED CHOCOLATE FUDGE CAKE

SERVES 6–8

4 ounces unsweetened chocolate, chopped into small pieces
¾ cup unsalted butter or margarine, softened
generous 1 cup light brown sugar
1 teaspoon vanilla extract
3 eggs, beaten
⅔ cup plain yogurt
1¼ cups self-rising flour
confectioners' sugar and chocolate curls, to decorate

FOR THE FROSTING

4 ounces dark chocolate, chopped into small pieces
¼ cup unsalted butter
2¼ cups confectioners' sugar
6 tablespoons plain yogurt

1 Preheat oven to 375°F. Lightly grease two 8-inch round cake pans and line the base of each with baking parchment. Melt the chocolate.

2 In a mixing bowl, cream the butter with the sugar until light and fluffy. Beat in the vanilla, then gradually add the beaten eggs, beating well after each addition.

3 Stir in the melted chocolate and yogurt evenly. Fold in the flour with a metal spoon.

4 Divide the mixture between the prepared pans. Bake for 25–30 minutes or until the cakes are firm to the touch. Turn onto a wire rack and let cool.

5 To make the frosting, melt the chocolate and butter in a saucepan over low heat. Remove from the heat and stir in the confectioners' sugar and yogurt. Mix with a rubber spatula until smooth, then beat until the frosting begins to cool and thicken slightly. Use about a third of the mixture to sandwich the cakes together.

6 Working quickly, spread the remainder over the top and sides. Sprinkle with the sugar and decorate with chocolate curls.

CHOCOLATE BRANDY SNAP CAKE

SERVES 8

8 ounces dark chocolate, chopped
1 cup unsalted butter, softened
generous 1 cup dark brown sugar
6 eggs, separated
1 teaspoon vanilla extract
1¼ cups ground hazelnuts
¼ cup fresh white bread crumbs
finely grated zest of 1 large orange
1 recipe Chocolate Ganache, for filling
and frosting (omit jelly)
confectioners' sugar, for dusting

FOR THE BRANDY SNAPS

¼ cup unsalted butter
¼ cup sugar
⅓ cup corn syrup
½ cup all-purpose flour
1 teaspoon brandy

1 Preheat oven to 350°F. Grease two
8-inch cake pans and line the base of each
with baking parchment. Melt the
chocolate and set aside to cool slightly.
2 Cream the butter with the sugar in a
mixing bowl until fluffy. Beat in the egg
yolks and vanilla. Add the chocolate and
mix thoroughly.
3 In a clean, grease-free bowl, whisk the
egg whites to soft peaks, then fold them
into the chocolate mixture with the
ground hazelnuts, bread crumbs and
orange zest.
4 Divide the cake mixture between the
prepared pans and spread evenly. Bake for
25–30 minutes or until springy and firm
to the touch. Turn over onto wire racks.
Leave the oven on.
5 Make the brandy snaps. Line two baking
sheets with baking parchment. Melt the
butter, sugar and syrup together.
6 Stir the butter mixture until smooth.
Remove from the heat and stir in the
flour and brandy.

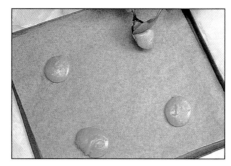

7 Place small spoonfuls of the mixture
well apart on the baking sheets and bake
for 8–10 minutes, until golden. Cool for
a few seconds until firm enough to lift
onto a wire rack.

8 Immediately pinch the edges of each
brandy snap to create a frilled effect. If
the cookies become too firm, soften them
briefly in the oven.
9 Sandwich the cake layers together with
half the chocolate ganache, transfer to a
plate and spread the remaining ganache
on the top. Arrange the brandy snaps over
the cake and dust with the sugar.

COOK'S TIP
To save time, you can use ready-
made brandy snaps. Simply warm
them for a few minutes in the oven
until they are pliable enough to
shape. Or use as they are, filling
them with cream, and arranging
them so that they fan out from the
center of the cake.

CHOCOLATE COCONUT ROULADE

4 Scrape the mixture into the prepared pan, taking it right into the corners. Smooth the surface with a metal spatula, then bake for 20–25 minutes or until firm and springy to the touch.

5 Turn the cooked roulade out onto the sugar-dusted wax paper and carefully peel off the lining paper. Cover with a damp, clean dish towel and let cool completely.

6 To make the filling, whisk the cream with the whiskey in a bowl until the mixture just holds it shape, grate the coconut cream and stir in with the sugar.

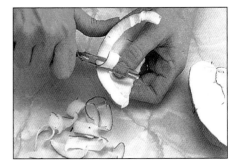

7 Uncover the sponge and spread about three-quarters of the cream mixture to the edges. Roll up carefully from a long side. Transfer to a plate, pipe or spoon the remaining cream mixture on top. Use a vegetable peeler to make coconut and chocolate curls to decorate the cake.

SERVES 8
½ cup sugar
5 eggs, separated
½ cup cocoa powder
FOR THE FILLING
1¼ cups heavy cream
3 tablespoons whiskey or brandy
2-ounce piece coconut cream
2 tablespoons sugar
FOR THE TOPPING
a piece of fresh coconut
dark chocolate for curls

1 Preheat oven to 350°F. Grease a 33 x 13 x 9-inch jelly roll pan. Lay a large sheet of wax paper or baking parchment on the work surface and dust it evenly with 2 tablespoons of the sugar.

2 Place the egg yolks in a heatproof bowl. Add the remaining sugar and whisk with a hand-held electric mixer until the mixture thickens. Sift in the cocoa, then fold in carefully and evenly with a metal spoon.

3 Whisk the egg whites in a clean, grease-free bowl until they form soft peaks. Fold about 1 tablespoon of the whites into the chocolate mixture to lighten it, then fold in the rest evenly.

WHITE CHOCOLATE CAPPUCCINO CAKE

SERVES 8

4 eggs
½ cup sugar
1 tablespoon strong black coffee
½ teaspoon vanilla extract
1 cup all-purpose flour
3 ounces white chocolate, coarsely grated
FOR THE FILLING
½ cup heavy cream
1 tablespoon coffee liqueur
FOR THE FROSTING AND TOPPING
1 tablespoon coffee liqueur
1 quantity Chocolate Frosting, using white chocolate and 2 cups confectioners' sugar
white chocolate curls
cocoa powder or ground cinnamon, for dusting

<u>1</u> Preheat oven to 350°F. Grease two 7-inch round cake pans and line the base of each with baking parchment.

<u>2</u> Combine the eggs, sugar, coffee and vanilla extract in a large heatproof bowl. Place over a saucepan of hot water and whisk until thick.

<u>3</u> Sift half the flour over the mixture; fold in gently and evenly. Fold in the remaining flour with the grated white chocolate.

<u>4</u> Divide the mixture between the prepared pans and spread evenly. Bake for 20–25 minutes, until firm and golden brown, then turn over onto wire racks and let cool completely.

<u>5</u> To make the filling, whip the cream with the coffee liqueur in a bowl until it holds its shape. Spread it over one of the cakes, then place the second layer on top.

<u>6</u> Stir the coffee liqueur into the frosting. Spread it over the top and sides of the cake, swirling with a palette knife. Top with curls of white chocolate and dust with cocoa or cinnamon. Transfer the cake to a serving plate and set aside until the frosting has set. Serve the cake on the day it is made, if possible.

WHITE CHOCOLATE CELEBRATION CAKE

SERVES 40–50

8 cups all-purpose flour
½ teaspoon salt
4 teaspoons baking soda
1 pound white chocolate, chopped
2 cups heavy cream
2 cups unsalted butter, softened
4 cups sugar
12 eggs
4 teaspoons lemon extract
grated zest of 2 lemons
1⅓ cups buttermilk
lemon curd, for filling
chocolate leaves, to decorate

FOR THE LEMON SYRUP
scant 1 cup sugar
1 cup water
¼ cup lemon juice

FOR THE BUTTERCREAM
1½ pounds white chocolate, chopped
2¼ pounds cream cheese, softened
2½ cups unsalted butter, at room temperature
¼ cup lemon juice
1 teaspoon lemon extract

1 Divide all the ingredients into two equal batches, so that the quantities are more manageable. Use each batch to make one cake. Preheat oven to 350°F. Grease a 12-inch round cake pan. Line with baking parchment. Sift the flour, salt and baking soda into a bowl and set aside. Melt the chocolate and cream in a saucepan over medium heat, stirring until smooth. Set aside to cool to room temperature.

VARIATION

For a summer celebration, decorate the cake with raspberries and white chocolate petals. To make the petals, you will need 3-inch foil squares. Spread melted white chocolate thinly over each piece of foil, so that it resembles a rose petal. Before the chocolate sets, bend the foil up to emphasize the petal shape. When set, remove the foil.

2 Beat the butter until creamy, then add the sugar and beat for 2–3 minutes. Beat in the eggs, then beat in the melted chocolate, lemon extract and zest. Gradually add the flour mixture, alternately with the buttermilk, to make a smooth pouring mixture. Pour into the pan and bake for 1 hour or until a toothpick inserted in the cake comes out clean.

3 Cool in the pan for 10 minutes, then turn the cake onto a wire rack and cool completely. Wrap in plastic wrap until ready to assemble. Using the second batch of ingredients, make another cake in the same way.

4 Make the lemon syrup. In a small saucepan, combine the sugar and water. Over a medium heat, bring to a boil, stirring until the sugar dissolves. Remove from the heat, stir in the lemon juice and cool completely. Store in an airtight container until required.

5 To make the buttercream, melt the chocolate. Cool slightly. Beat the cream cheese in a bowl until smooth. Gradually beat in the cooled white chocolate, then the butter, lemon juice and extract. Chill.

6 Split each cake in half. Spoon syrup over each layer, let it soak in, then repeat. Spread the bottom half of each cake with lemon curd and replace the tops.

7 Gently beat the buttercream in a bowl until creamy. Spread a quarter over the top of one of the filled cakes. Place the second filled cake on top. Spread a small amount of softened butter over the top and sides of the cake to create a smooth, crumb-free surface. Chill for 15 minutes, so the buttercream sets a little.

8 Place the cake on a serving plate. Set aside a quarter of the remaining buttercream for piping, then spread the rest evenly over the top and sides of the filled cake.

9 Spoon the reserved buttercream into a large icing bag fitted with a small star tip. Pipe a shell pattern around the rim of the cake. Decorate with chocolate leaves, made with dark or white chocolate (or a mixture) and fresh flowers.

Rich Chocolate Leaf Cake

Serves 8

3 ounces dark chocolate, broken into squares
⅔ cup milk
¾ cup unsalted butter, softened
1⅓ cups light brown sugar
3 eggs
2¼ cups all-purpose flour
2 teaspoons baking powder
5 tablespoons half-and-half

For the Filling and Topping

¼ cup raspberry preserves
1 recipe Chocolate Ganache
dark and white chocolate leaves

1 Preheat oven to 375°F. Grease and line two 8½-inch sandwich cake pans. Melt the chocolate with the milk over a low heat and let cool slightly.

2 Cream the butter with the sugar in a mixing bowl until light and fluffy. Add the eggs, one at a time, beating well after each addition.

3 Sift the flour and baking powder over the mixture and fold in gently but thoroughly. Stir in the chocolate mixture and the cream, mixing until smooth. Divide between the prepared pans and spread evenly.

4 Bake the cakes for 30–35 minutes or until they are springy and firm to the touch. Cool in the pans for a few minutes, then turn out onto wire racks.

5 Sandwich the cake layers together with the raspberry preserves. Spread the chocolate ganache over the cake and swirl with a knife. Place the cake on a serving plate, then decorate with the chocolate leaves.

CARIBBEAN CHOCOLATE RING WITH RUM SYRUP

SERVES 8–10

½ cup unsalted butter

¾ cup light brown sugar

2 eggs, beaten

2 ripe bananas, mashed

2 tablespoons shredded coconut

2 tablespoons sour cream

1 cup self-rising flour

3 tablespoons cocoa powder

½ teaspoon baking soda

FOR THE SYRUP

½ cup sugar

2 tablespoons dark rum

2 ounces unsweetened dark chocolate, chopped

TO DECORATE

mixture of tropical fruits, such as mango, papaya, starfruit and gooseberries

chocolate shapes or curls

1 Preheat oven to 350°F. Grease a 6¼-cup ring pan with butter.

2 Cream the butter and sugar in a bowl until light and fluffy. Add the eggs gradually, beating well, then mix in the bananas, coconut and sour cream.

3 Sift the flour, cocoa and baking soda over the mixture and fold in thoroughly and evenly.

4 Pour into the prepared pan and spread evenly. Bake for 45–50 minutes, until firm to the touch. Cool for 10 minutes in the pan, then turn over onto a wire rack to cool completely.

5 For the syrup, place the sugar in a small pan. Add 1 quarter cup water and heat gently, stirring occasionally until dissolved. Bring to a rapid boil, without stirring, for 2 minutes. Remove from the heat.

6 Add the rum and chocolate to the syrup and stir until the mixture is melted and smooth, then spoon evenly over the top and sides of the cake.

7 Decorate the ring with tropical fruit and chocolate shapes or curls.

White Chocolate Mousse and Strawberry Layer Cake

4 Make the mousse filling. In a medium saucepan over a low heat, melt the chocolate and cream until smooth, stirring frequently. Stir in the rum or strawberry-flavored liqueur and pour into a bowl. Chill until just set. With a wire whisk, whip lightly.

Serves 10

4 ounces white chocolate, chopped into small pieces
½ cup heavy cream
½ cup milk
1 tablespoon rum or vanilla extract
½ cup unsalted butter, softened
¾ cup sugar
3 eggs
2 cups all-purpose flour
2 teaspoons baking powder
pinch of salt
1½ pounds fresh strawberries, sliced, plus extra for decoration
3 cups heavy cream
2 tablespoons rum or strawberry-flavored liqueur

White Chocolate Mousse Filling

9 ounces white chocolate, chopped into small pieces
1½ cups heavy cream
2 tablespoons rum or strawberry-flavored liqueur

1 Preheat oven to 350°F. Grease and flour two 9-inch cake pans. Line the base of the pans with baking parchment. Melt the chocolate and cream in a double boiler over low heat, stirring until smooth. Stir in the milk and rum, and set aside to cool.

2 In a large mixing bowl, beat the butter and sugar with a hand-held electric mixer for 3–5 minutes, until light and creamy, scraping the sides of the bowl occasionally. Add the eggs one at a time, beating well after each addition. In a small bowl, stir together the flour, baking powder and salt. Alternately add flour and melted chocolate to the egg mixture in batches, until just blended. Pour the mixture into the pans and spread evenly.

3 Bake for 20–25 minutes, until a toothpick inserted in the cake comes out clean. Cool in the pan for 10 minutes, then turn cakes out onto a wire rack, peel off the paper and cool completely.

5 Assemble the cake. With a serrated knife, slice both cake layers in half, making four layers. Place one layer on the plate and spread one third of the mousse on top. Arrange one third of the sliced strawberries over the mousse. Place the second layer on top and spread with another third of the mousse. Arrange another third of the sliced strawberries over the mousse. Place the third layer on top and spread with the remaining mousse. Cover with the remaining sliced strawberries. Top with the last cake layer.

6 Whip the cream with the rum until firm peaks form. Spread about half the whipped cream over the top and the sides of the cake. Spoon the remaining cream into a decorating bag fitted with a medium star tip and pipe scrolls on top of the cake. Decorate with the remaining sliced strawberries, pressing half of them into the cream on the sides of the cake and arranging the rest on top.

CHOCOLATE CHESTNUT ROULADE

SERVES 10–12

6 ounces bittersweet chocolate, chopped
into small pieces
2 tablespoons cocoa powder, sifted
¼ cup hot strong coffee or espresso
6 eggs, separated
6 tablespoons sugar
pinch of cream of tartar
1 teaspoon pure vanilla extract
cocoa powder, for dusting
candied chestnuts, to decorate
CHESTNUT CREAM FILLING
2 cups heavy cream
2 tablespoons rum or coffee-flavored liqueur
1½ cups canned sweetened chestnut purée
4 ounces bittersweet chocolate, grated

4 Dust a dish towel with cocoa. Turn the cake out onto the towel immediately and remove the paper. Trim off any crisp edges. Starting at a narrow end, roll the cake and towel together jelly-roll fashion. Cool completely.

5 To make the filling, whip the cream and rum or liqueur until soft peaks form. Beat a spoonful of cream into the chestnut purée to lighten it, then fold in the remaining cream and grated chocolate. Set aside a quarter of this mixture for the decoration. Unroll the cake and spread chestnut cream to within 1 inch of the edge.

6 Using a dish towel to lift the cake, carefully roll it up again. Place seam-side down on a serving plate. Spread some of the reserved chestnut cream over the top and use the rest for piped rosettes. Decorate with the candied chestnuts.

1 Preheat oven to 350°F. Lightly grease the base and sides of a 15½ x 10½ x 1-inch jelly roll pan. Line with baking parchment, allowing a 1-inch overhang. Melt the chocolate. Dissolve the cocoa in the hot coffee to make a paste. Set aside.

2 Using a hand-held mixer, beat the egg yolks with half the sugar in a mixing bowl until thick and foamy. Slowly beat in the melted chocolate and cocoa-coffee paste until just blended. In a separate bowl, beat the egg whites and cream of tartar until stiff peaks form. Sprinkle the remaining sugar over the whites in two batches and beat until the whites are stiff and glossy, then beat in the vanilla extract.

3 Stir a spoonful of the whites into the chocolate mixture to lighten it, then fold in the rest. Spoon into the pan. Bake for 20–25 minutes or until the cake springs back when touched with a fingertip.

CHOCOLATE RED CURRANT TORTE

SERVES 8–10

½ cup unsalted butter, softened

⅔ cup dark brown sugar

2 eggs

⅔ cup sour cream

1¼ cups self-rising flour

1 teaspoon baking powder

½ cup cocoa powder

¾ cup stemmed red currants, plus

1 cup red currant sprigs, to decorate

FOR THE ICING

5 ounces plain chocolate, chopped into small pieces

3 tablespoons red currant jelly

2 tablespoons dark rum

½ cup heavy cream

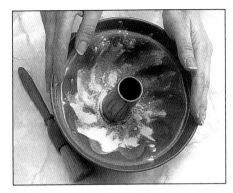

1 Preheat oven to 350°F. Grease a 5-cup ring pan and dust lightly with flour. Cream the butter with the sugar in a mixing bowl until light and fluffy. Beat in the eggs and sour cream until thoroughly mixed.

2 Sift the flour, baking powder and cocoa over the mixture, then fold in lightly and evenly. Fold in the red currants. Spoon the mixture into the prepared pan and spread evenly. Bake for 40–50 minutes or until springy and firm to the touch. Turn out onto a wire rack and let cool completely.

3 To make the icing, mix the chocolate, red currant jelly and rum in a heatproof bowl. Set the bowl over simmering water and heat gently, stirring occasionally, until melted. Remove from the heat and cool to room temperature, then add the cream, a little at a time. Mix well.

4 Transfer the cooked cake to a serving plate. Spoon the icing evenly over the cake, letting it drizzle down the sides. Decorate with red currant sprigs just before serving.

COOK'S TIP

Use a decorative gugelhupf tin or mold, if you have one. When preparing it, add a little cocoa powder to the flour used for dusting the greased pan, to prevent the cooked chocolate cake from being streaked with white.

CHOCOLATE BOX WITH CARAMEL MOUSSE AND BERRIES

SERVES 8–10

*10 ounces unsweetened chocolate, chopped into
small pieces*

FOR THE CARAMEL MOUSSE

*4 x 2 ounces chocolate-coated caramel bars,
coarsely chopped*

1½ tablespoons milk or water

1½ cups heavy cream

1 egg white

FOR THE CARAMEL SHARDS

½ cup sugar

¼ cup water

FOR THE TOPPING

*4 ounces white chocolate, chopped into small
pieces*

1½ cups heavy cream

*1 pound mixed berries or cut-up fruits such as
raspberries, strawberries, blackberries or sliced
nectarine and orange segments*

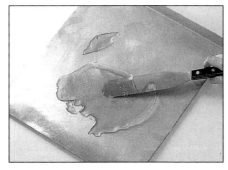

1 Prepare the chocolate box. Turn a 9-inch square baking pan bottom side up. Mold a piece of foil around the pan, then turn it right side up and line it with the foil, pressing against the edges to make the foil as smooth as possible.

2 Place the chocolate in a heatproof bowl over a saucepan of simmering water. Stir until the chocolate has melted and is smooth. Immediately pour the melted chocolate into the lined pan. Tilt to coat the bottom and sides evenly, keeping the top edges of the sides as straight as possible. As the chocolate coats the sides, tilt the pan again to coat the corners and sides once more. Chill until firm.

3 Place the caramel bars and milk or water in a heatproof bowl. Place over a pan of simmering water and stir until melted. Remove the bowl from the heat and cool for 10 minutes, stirring occasionally.

4 Using a hand-held electric mixer, whip the cream in a bowl until soft peaks form. Stir a spoonful of the whipped cream into the caramel mixture to lighten it, then fold in the remaining cream. In another bowl beat the egg white until just stiff. Fold the egg white into the mousse mixture. Pour into the box. Chill for several hours or overnight, until set.

5 Meanwhile, make the caramel shards. Lightly oil a baking sheet. In a small pan over a low heat, dissolve the sugar in the water, swirling the pan gently. Increase the heat and boil the mixture for 4–5 minutes, until the sugar begins to turn a pale golden color. Protecting your hand with an oven mitt, immediately pour the mixture onto the oiled sheet. Tilt the sheet to distribute the caramel in an even layer. (*Do not touch – caramel is dangerously hot.*) Cool completely, then using a metal spatula, lift the caramel off the baking sheet and break into pieces.

6 Make the topping. Combine the white chocolate and ½ cup of the cream in a small pan and melt over a low heat until smooth, stirring frequently. Strain into a medium bowl and cool to room temperature, stirring occasionally. In another bowl, beat the remaining cream with a hand-held electric mixer, until firm peaks form. Stir a spoonful of cream into the white chocolate mixture, then gently fold in the remaining whipped cream.

7 Using the foil as a guide, remove the mousse-filled box from the pan and peel the foil carefully from the sides, then the bottom. Slide the box gently onto a serving plate.

8 Spoon the chocolate-cream mixture into a piping bag fitted with a medium star tip. Pipe a decorative design of rosettes or shells over the surface of the set mousse. Decorate the cream-topped box with the mixed berries or cut-up fruits and the caramel shards.

HOT
DESSERTS

DARK CHOCOLATE RAVIOLI WITH WHITE CHOCOLATE AND CREAM CHEESE FILLING

SERVES 4

1½ cups all-purpose flour
¼ cup cocoa powder
2 tablespoons confectioners' sugar
2 large eggs, beaten
1 tablespoon olive oil
salt
half-and-half and grated chocolate, to serve
FOR THE FILLING
6 ounces white chocolate, chopped
3 cups cream cheese
1 egg, plus 1 beaten egg to seal

1 To make the pasta, sift the flour with the cocoa and confectioners' sugar onto a work surface. Make a well in the center and pour in the eggs and oil. Combine with your fingers. Knead until smooth. Alternatively, make the dough in a food processor, then knead by hand. Cover and let sit for at least 30 minutes.

2 To make the filling, melt the white chocolate in a heatproof bowl placed over a pan of simmering water. Cool slightly. Beat the cream cheese in a bowl, then beat in the chocolate and egg. Spoon into a piping bag fitted with a plain nozzle.

3 Cut the dough in half and wrap one portion in plastic wrap. Roll the pasta out thinly into a rectangle on a lightly floured surface, or use a pasta machine. Cover with a clean damp dish towel and repeat with the remaining pasta.

4 Pipe small 1-teaspoon mounds of filling in even rows, spacing them at 1½-inch intervals across one piece of the dough. Using a pastry brush, brush the spaces of dough between the mounds with beaten egg.

5 Using a rolling pin, lift the remaining sheet of pasta over the dough with the filling. Press down firmly between the pockets of filling, pushing out any trapped air. Cut the filled chocolate pasta into rounds with a serrated ravioli cutter or sharp knife. Transfer to a floured dish towel. Let dry for 1 hour, until ready for cooking.

6 Bring a frying pan of water to a boil and add the ravioli a few at a time, stirring to prevent them from sticking together. (Adding a few drops of vegetable oil to the water will help, too.) Simmer gently for 3–5 minutes, remove with a perforated spoon and serve with a generous splash of light cream and grated chocolate.

Chocolate Almond Meringue Pie

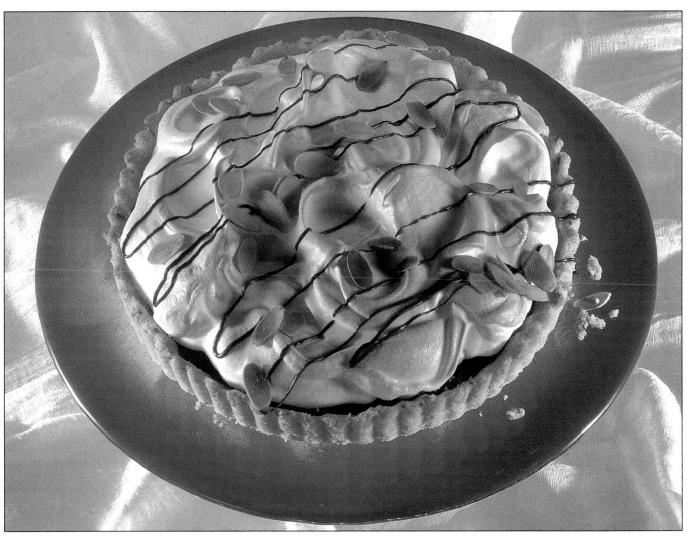

Serves 6

1½ cups all-purpose flour

½ cup ground rice

⅔ cup unsalted butter

finely grated zest of 1 orange

1 egg yolk

flaked almonds and melted dark chocolate, to decorate

For the Filling

5 ounces dark chocolate, chopped into small pieces

¼ cup unsalted butter, softened

6 tablespoons sugar

2 teaspoons cornstarch

4 egg yolks

¾ cup ground almonds

For the Meringue

3 egg whites

⅔ cup sugar·

1 Sift the flour and ground rice into a bowl. Rub in the butter until the mixture resembles bread crumbs. Stir in the orange zest. Add the egg yolk; bring the dough together. Roll out and use to line a 9-inch round flan pan. Chill.

2 Preheat oven to 375°F. Prick the pastry base, cover with wax paper weighed down with baking stones and bake blind for 10 minutes.

3 Make the filling. Melt the chocolate, then cream the butter with the sugar in a bowl, and beat in the cornstarch and egg yolks. Fold in the almonds, then the melted chocolate. Remove the paper and stones from the pastry case and add the filling. Bake for another 10 minutes.

4 Make the meringue. Whisk the egg whites in a clean, grease-free bowl until stiff, then gradually whisk in about half the sugar. Fold in the remaining sugar with a metal spoon.

5 Spoon the meringue over the chocolate filling, lifting it up with the back of the spoon to form peaks. Reduce the oven temperature to 350°F and bake the pie for 15–20 minutes or until the topping is golden. Serve warm, sprinkled with the almonds and drizzled with the melted chocolate.

MAGIC CHOCOLATE MUD PUDDING

SERVES 4

¼ cup butter, plus extra for greasing
scant 1 cup self-rising flour
1 teaspoon ground cinnamon
5 tablespoons cocoa powder
1 cup light brown sugar
2 cups milk
crème fraîche, plain yogurt or vanilla
ice cream, to serve

1 Preheat oven to 350°F. Prepare the dish: use the extra butter to grease a 6-cup ovenproof dish. Place the dish on a baking sheet and set aside.

2 Sift the flour and ground cinnamon into a bowl. Sift in 1 tablespoon of the cocoa and mix well.

3 Place the butter in a saucepan. Add ½ cup of the sugar and ⅔ cup of the milk. Heat gently without boiling, stirring occasionally, until the butter has melted and all the sugar has dissolved. Remove the pan from the heat.

4 Stir in the flour mixture, mixing evenly. Pour the mixture into the prepared dish and spread evenly.

5 Mix the remaining sugar and cocoa in a bowl, then sprinkle on the pudding mixture.

6 Pour the remaining milk evenly over the pudding.

7 Bake for 45–50 minutes or until the sponge is springy and firm to the touch. Serve hot, with the crème fraîche, yogurt or ice cream.

Chocolate Crêpes with Plums and Port

2 Meanwhile, make the filling. Halve and pit the plums. Place them in a saucepan and add the sugar and water. Bring to a boil, then lower the heat, cover, and simmer for about 10 minutes or until the plums are tender. Stir in the port, taking care not to break up the plums, then simmer for 30 more seconds. Remove from the heat and keep warm.

3 Have ready a sheet of baking parchment. Heat a crêpe pan, grease it lightly with a little oil, then pour in just enough batter to cover the base of the pan, swirling to coat evenly. Cook until the crêpe has set, then flip it over to cook the other side. Slide the crêpe out onto the sheet of paper, then cook 9–11 more crêpes in the same way. It should not be necessary to add more oil to the pan, but if the crêpes start to stick, add a very light coating.

4 To make the sauce, combine the chocolate and cream in a saucepan. Heat gently, stirring until smooth. Add the port and heat gently, stirring, for one minute.

5 Divide the plum filling among the crêpes, add a dollop of crème fraîche or plain yogurt to each and roll them up carefully. Serve in individual bowls, with the chocolate sauce spooned over the top of each portion.

Serves 6

2 ounces unsweetened chocolate, chopped into
small pieces
1 cup milk
½ cup light cream
2 tablespoons cocoa powder
1 cup all-purpose flour
2 eggs
oil, for frying

For the Filling

1¼ pounds red or golden plums
¼ cup sugar
2 tablespoons water
2 tablespoons port
¾ cup crème fraîche or
plain yogurt

For the Sauce

5 ounces unsweetened chocolate, chopped into
small pieces
¾ cup heavy cream
1 tablespoon port

1 Make the crêpe batter. Place the chocolate in a saucepan with the milk. Heat gently, stirring occasionally, until the chocolate has dissolved. Pour the chocolate and milk mixture into a blender or food processor and add the cream, cocoa, flour and eggs. (If the blender or food processor is a small one, it may be necessary to do this in batches.) Process until smooth, then pour into a bowl and chill for 30 minutes.

Steamed Chocolate and Fruit Puddings with Chocolate Syrup

Serves 4

²/₃ cup dark brown sugar
1 apple
³/₄ cup cranberries, thawed if frozen
¹/₂ cup soft margarine
2 eggs
¹/₂ cup self-rising flour
3 tablespoons cocoa powder

For the Chocolate Syrup

4 ounces unsweetened chocolate, chopped
2 tablespoons honey
1 tablespoon unsalted butter
¹/₂ teaspoon vanilla extract

1 Prepare a steamer or half fill a saucepan with water and bring to a boil. Grease four individual deep bowls and sprinkle each one with a little of the brown sugar to coat well all over.

2 Peel and core the apple. Dice it into a bowl, add the cranberries and mix well. Divide the fruit among the prepared deep bowls.

3 Place the remaining brown sugar in a mixing bowl. Add the margarine, eggs, flour and cocoa. Beat until combined and smooth.

4 Spoon the mixture into the bowls and cover each with a double thickness of foil. Steam for about 45 minutes, adding more boiling water as required, until the puddings are puffed up and firm.

5 To make the syrup, mix the chocolate, honey, butter and vanilla in a small saucepan. Heat gently, stirring until melted and smooth.

6 Run a knife around the edge of each pudding to loosen it, then turn over onto individual plates. Serve immediately, with the chocolate syrup.

Chocolate Soufflé Crêpes

Makes 12 crepes

¾ cup all-purpose flour

1 tablespoon cocoa powder

1 teaspoon sugar

pinch of salt

1 teaspoon ground cinnamon

2 eggs

¾ cup milk

1 teaspoon vanilla extract

¼ cup unsalted butter, melted

confectioners' sugar, for dusting

raspberries, pineapple and mint sprigs,
to decorate

For the Pineapple Syrup

½ medium pineapple, peeled, cored and
finely chopped

½ cup water

2 tablespoons pure maple syrup

1 teaspoon cornstarch

½ cinnamon stick

2 tablespoons rum

For the Soufflé Filling

9 ounces bittersweet chocolate, chopped into
small pieces

⅓ cup heavy cream

3 eggs, separated

2 tablespoons sugar

1 Prepare the syrup. In a saucepan over medium heat, bring the pineapple, water, maple syrup, cornstarch and cinnamon stick to a boil. Simmer for 2–3 minutes, until the sauce thickens, whisking frequently. Remove from the heat and discard the cinnamon. Pour into a bowl, and stir in the rum. Cool, then chill.

Cook's Tip
You might be able to find ready-made crêpes at food specialty store, which will save time.

2 Prepare the crêpes. Sift the flour, cocoa, sugar, salt and cinnamon into a bowl. Stir, then make a well in the center. In a bowl, beat the eggs, milk and vanilla. Gradually add to the well in the flour mixture, whisking in flour from the side of the bowl to form a smooth batter. Stir in half the melted butter and pour into a pitcher. Let stand for one hour.

3 Heat a 7–8-inch crêpe pan. Brush with butter. Stir the batter. Pour 3 tablespoons batter into the pan; swirl the pan to cover the bottom. Cook over medium-high heat for 1–2 minutes, until the bottom is golden. Turn over and cook for 30–45 seconds, then turn onto a plate. Stack between sheets of baking parchment and set aside.

4 Prepare the filling. In a saucepan over medium heat, melt the chocolate and cream until smooth, stirring frequently.

5 In a bowl, with a hand-held electric mixer, beat the yolks with half the sugar for 3–5 minutes, until light and creamy. Gradually beat in the chocolate mixture. Let cool. In a separate bowl with clean beaters, beat the egg whites until soft peaks form. Gradually beat in the remaining sugar until stiff peaks form. Beat a large spoonful of whites into the chocolate mixture to lighten it, then fold in the remaining whites.

6 Preheat oven to 400°F. Lay a crêpe on a plate, bottom side up. Spoon a little soufflé mixture onto the crêpe, spreading it to the edge. Fold the bottom half over the soufflé mixture, then fold in half again to form a filled triangle. Place on a buttered baking sheet. Repeat with the remaining crêpes. Brush the tops with melted butter and bake for 15–20 minutes, until the filling has souffléd. Dust with the sugar and decorate with raspberries, pineapple pieces and mint. Serve with the syrup.

Variation
For a simpler version of the crêpes, just serve with a spoonful of maple syrup rather than making the pineapple syrup.

Chocolate and Orange Scotch Crêpes

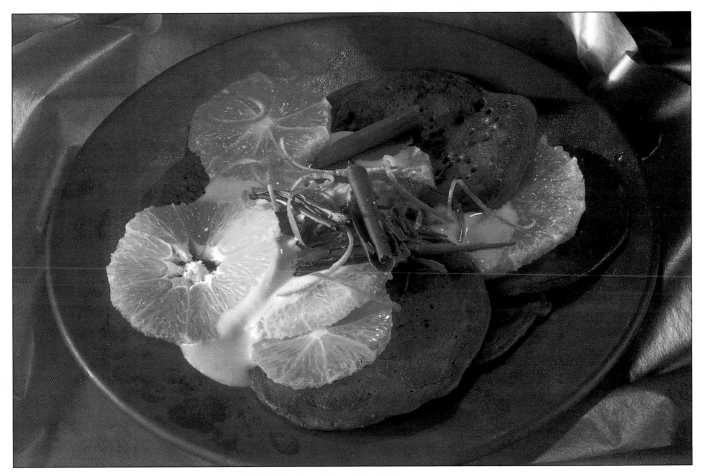

Serves 4

1 cup self-rising flour
2 tablespoons cocoa powder
2 eggs
2 ounces unsweetened chocolate, chopped into small pieces
1 cup milk
finely grated zest of 1 orange
2 tablespoons orange juice
butter or oil, for frying
chocolate curls, to decorate

For the Sauce

2 large oranges
2 tablespoons unsalted butter
3 tablespoons light brown sugar
1 cup crème fraîche
2 tablespoons Grand Marnier or Cointreau

1 Sift the flour and cocoa into a bowl and make a well in the center. Add the eggs and beat well, gradually incorporating the surrounding dry ingredients to make a smooth mixture.

2 Mix the chocolate and milk in a saucepan. Heat gently until the chocolate has melted, then beat into the mixture until smooth and bubbly. Stir in the orange zest and juice to make a batter.

3 Heat a large heavy frying pan or griddle. Grease with a little butter or oil. Drop large spoonfuls of batter onto the hot surface, leaving room for spreading. Cook over moderate heat. When the pancakes are lightly browned underneath and bubbly on top, flip over to cook the other side. Slide onto a plate and keep hot, as you continue to make more crêpes.

4 Make the sauce. Grate the zest of one orange into a bowl and set aside. Peel both oranges, taking care to remove all the pith, then slice the fruit thin.

5 Heat the butter and sugar in a wide, shallow pan over low heat, stirring until the sugar dissolves. Stir in the crème fraîche and heat gently.

6 Add the pancakes and orange slices to the sauce, heat gently for 1–2 minutes, then spoon on the liqueur. Sprinkle with the reserved orange zest. Sprinkle on the chocolate curls and serve the crêpes immediately.

PUFFY PEARS

SERVES 4

8 ounces puff pastry, thawed if frozen
2 pears, peeled
2 squares unsweetened chocolate, roughly chopped
1 tablespoon lemon juice
1 egg, beaten
1 tablespoon sugar

<u>1</u> Roll the pastry into a 10-inch square on a lightly floured surface. Trim the edges, then cut it into four equal smaller squares. Cover with plastic wrap and set aside.

<u>2</u> Remove the core from each pear half and fill the cavity with the chopped chocolate. Place a pear half, cut side down, on each piece of pastry and brush them with the lemon juice, to prevent them from turning brown.

<u>3</u> Preheat oven to 375°F. Cut the pastry into a pear shape, by following the lines of the fruit, leaving a 1-inch border. Use the trimmings to make leaves and brush the pastry border with the beaten egg.

<u>4</u> Arrange the pastry and pears on a baking sheet. Make deep cuts in the pears, taking care not to cut right through the fruit, and sprinkle them with the sugar. Cook for 20–25 minutes, until lightly browned. Serve hot or cold.

VARIATION

Use apples instead of pears, if preferred. Cut the pastry into 4-inch rounds. Slice 2 peeled and cored apples. Toss with a little lemon juice, drain and arrange on the pastry. Dot with 2 tablespoons butter and chopped milk chocolate. Bake as for Puffy Pears.
While still hot, brush the apple slices with warmed red currant jelly.

PEARS IN CHOCOLATE FUDGE BLANKETS

SERVES 6

6 ripe pears
2 tablespoons lemon juice
6 tablespoons sugar
1 ¼ cups water
1 cinnamon stick
FOR THE SAUCE
1 cup heavy cream
1 cup light brown sugar
2 tablespoons unsalted butter
2 tablespoons corn syrup
½ cup milk
7 ounces unsweetened dark chocolate, broken into squares

<u>1</u> Peel the pears, leaving the stalks on. Scoop out the cores from the base. Brush the cut surfaces with lemon juice to prevent them from browning.

<u>2</u> Place the sugar and water in a large saucepan. Heat gently until the sugar dissolves. Add the pears and cinnamon stick with any remaining lemon juice, and, if necessary, a little more water, so the pears are almost covered.

<u>3</u> Bring to a boil, then lower the heat, cover the pan and simmer the pears gently for 15–20 minutes or until they are just tender when pierced with a skewer.

<u>4</u> Meanwhile, make the sauce. Place the cream, sugar, butter, corn syrup and milk in a heavy saucepan. Heat gently until the sugar has dissolved and the butter and syrup have melted, then bring to a boil. Boil, stirring constantly, for about 5 minutes or until the sauce is thick. Remove from the heat and stir in the chocolate, a few squares at a time, until melted.

<u>5</u> Using a slotted spoon, transfer the poached pears to a dish. Keep hot. Boil the syrup rapidly to reduce to about 3–4 tablespoons. Remove the cinnamon stick and stir the syrup into the chocolate sauce. Pour the sauce over the pears and serve in individual bowls.

TARTS, PIES & CHEESECAKES

RICH CHOCOLATE BERRY TART WITH BLACKBERRY SAUCE

SERVES 10

½ cup unsalted butter, softened

½ cup sugar

½ teaspoon salt

1 tablespoon vanilla extract

½ cup cocoa powder

1½ cups all-purpose flour

1 pound fresh berries, for topping

FOR THE CHOCOLATE GANACHE FILLING

2 cups heavy cream

½ cup blackberry or raspberry jelly

8 ounces bittersweet chocolate, chopped into small pieces

2 tablespoons unsalted butter, cut into small pieces

FOR THE BLACKBERRY SAUCE

8 ounces fresh or frozen blackberries or raspberries

1 tablespoon lemon juice

2 tablespoons sugar

2 tablespoons blackberry- or raspberry-flavored liqueur

1 In a food processor fitted with a metal blade, process the butter, sugar, salt and vanilla until creamy. Add the cocoa and process for one minute. Add the flour all at once, then pulse for 10–15 seconds. Place a piece of plastic wrap on the work surface. Turn the dough out onto this, shape into a flat disk and wrap tightly. Chill for one hour.

2 Lightly grease a 9-inch flan pan with a removable base. Let the dough soften for 5–10 minutes, then roll out between two sheets of plastic wrap to an 11-inch round, about ¼ inch thick. Peel off the top sheet of plastic wrap and invert the dough into the prepared pan. Ease the dough into the pan and, when in position, lift off the plastic wrap.

3 With floured fingers, press the dough onto the base and sides of the pan, then roll the rolling pin over the edge to cut off any excess dough. Prick the base of the dough with a fork. Chill for 1 hour. Preheat oven to 350°F. Line the pastry shell with baking parchment; fill with baking stones and bake blind for 10 minutes. Remove the paper and stones and bake for 5 more minutes, until the pastry is just set. Cool in the pan on a wire rack.

4 Prepare the ganache filling. In a medium saucepan over medium heat, bring the cream and berry jelly to the boil. Remove from the heat and add the chocolate all at once, stirring until melted and smooth. Stir in the butter until melted, then strain into the cooled tart shell, smoothing the top. Cool the tart completely.

5 Prepare the sauce. Process the berries, lemon juice and sugar in a food processor until smooth. Strain into a small bowl and add the liqueur.

6 To serve, remove the tart from the pan. Place on a serving plate and arrange the berries on top of the tart. With a pastry brush, brush the berries with a little of the blackberry sauce to glaze lightly. Serve the remaining sauce separately.

CHOCOLATE TRUFFLE TART

SERVES 12

1 cup all-purpose flour
⅓ cup cocoa powder
¼ cup sugar
½ teaspoon salt
½ cup unsalted butter, cut into pieces
1 egg yolk
1–2 tablespoons ice water
1 ounce white or milk chocolate, melted
heavy cream for serving (optional)
FOR THE TRUFFLE FILLING
1½ cups heavy cream
12 ounces couverture or bittersweet chocolate, chopped
¼ cup unsalted butter, cut into small pieces
2 tablespoons brandy or liqueur

1 Prepare the pastry. Sift the flour and cocoa into a bowl. In a food processor fitted with a metal blade, process the flour mixture with the sugar and salt. Add the butter and process for 15–20 seconds, until the mixture resembles coarse bread crumbs.

2 In a bowl, lightly beat the yolk with the ice water. Add to the flour mixture and pulse until the dough begins to stick together. Turn out the dough onto a sheet of plastic wrap. Use the film to help shape the dough into a flat disk. Wrap tightly. Chill for 1–2 hours, until firm.

3 Lightly grease a 9-inch tart pan with a removable base. Let the dough soften briefly, then roll it out between sheets of waxed paper or plastic wrap to an 11-inch round, about ¼ inch thick. Peel off the top sheet and invert the dough into a tart pan. Remove the bottom sheet. Ease the dough into the pan. Prick with a fork. Chill for one hour.

4 Preheat the oven to 350°F. Line the tart with foil or baking parchment; fill with baking stones. Bake blind for 5–7 minutes. Lift out the foil with the stones. return the pastry shell to the oven and bake for 5–7 more minutes, until the pastry is just set. Cool completely in the pan on a rack.

5 To prepare the filling, in a medium pan over medium heat, bring the cream to a boil. Remove the pan from the heat and stir in the chocolate until melted and smooth. Stir in the butter and brandy. Strain into the prepared tart shell, tilting the pan slightly to level the surface. Do not touch the surface of the filling or it will spoil the glossy finish.

6 Spoon the melted chocolate into a paper piping bag and cut off the tip. Drop rounds of chocolate over the surface of the tart and use a skewer or toothpick to draw a point gently through the chocolate to produce a marbled effect. Chill for 2–3 hours, until set. To serve, let the tart soften slightly at room temperature.

MARBLED CHEESECAKE

SERVES 6

½ cup cocoa powder

5 tablespoons hot water

2 pounds cream cheese, at room temperature

1 cup sugar

4 eggs

1 teaspoon vanilla extract

3 ounces graham crackers, crushed

1 Preheat oven to 350°F. Line an 8-inch cake pan with wax paper. Grease the paper.

2 Sift the cocoa powder into a bowl. Pour in the hot water and stir to dissolve.

3 Beat the cheese until smooth, then beat in the sugar, followed by the eggs, one at a time. Do not overmix.

4 Divide the mixture evenly between two bowls. Stir the chocolate mixture into one bowl, then add the vanilla to the remaining mixture.

5 Pour a cup or ladleful of the cream cheese mixture into the center of the pan; it will spread out into an even layer. Slowly pour a cupful of chocolate mixture into the center. Continue to alternate the cake mixtures in this way until both are used up. Draw a thin metal skewer through the cake mixture for a marbled effect.

6 Set the cake pan in a roasting pan and pour in hot water to come 1½ inches up the sides of the cake pan.

7 Bake the cheesecake for about 1½ hours, until the top is golden. (The cake will rise during baking but will sink later.) Cool in the pan on a wire rack.

8 Run a knife around the inside edge of the cake. Invert a flat plate over the pan and turn out the cake.

9 Sprinkle the crushed cookies evenly over the cake, gently invert another plate on top, and turn over again. Cover and chill for 3 hours, preferably overnight.

BLACK BOTTOM PIE

SERVES 6–8

2¼ cups all-purpose flour

⅔ cup unsalted butter

2 egg yolks

1–2 tablespoons ice water

FOR THE FILLING

3 eggs, separated

4 teaspoons cornstarch

6 tablespoons sugar

1⅔ cups milk

5 ounces unsweetened chocolate, chopped into
small pieces

1 teaspoon vanilla extract

1 envelope powdered gelatin

3 tablespoons water

2 tablespoons dark rum

FOR THE TOPPING

¾ cup heavy cream

chocolate curls

1 Sift the flour into a bowl and rub in the butter until the mixture resembles coarse bread crumbs. Stir in the egg yolks with just enough ice water to bind the mixture to a soft dough. Roll out on a lightly floured surface and line a deep 9-inch flan pan. Chill the pastry shell for about 30 minutes.

2 Preheat oven to 375°F. Prick the pastry shell all over with a fork, cover with wax paper weighed down with baking stones and bake blind for 10 minutes. Remove the baking stones and paper, return the pastry shell to the oven and bake 10 more minutes, until the pastry is crisp and golden. Cool in the pan.

POTS AU CHOCOLAT

The chocolate and chestnut mixture (minus the pastry) also makes delicious individual *pots au chocolat*. Make the fillings as described above; then simply pour the mixture into small ramekins that have been lightly greased with butter. Decorate with a dollop of whipped cream and grated chocolate and serve with *langues de chat*.

CHOCOLATE AND CHESTNUT PIE

9 inch pastry shell (see preceeding
recipe), cooked

FOR THE FILLING

½ cup butter, softened

¼ cup sugar

1 can (15 ounces) unsweetened chestnut
purée

8 ounces unsweetened chocolate, broken
into small pieces

2 tablespoons brandy

1 Make the filling. Cream the butter with the sugar in a mixing bowl until fluffy. Add the unsweetened chestnut purée, about 2 tablespoons at a time, beating well after each addition.

2 Put the chocolate in a heatproof bowl. Place over a saucepan of barely simmering water until the chocolate has melted, stirring occasionally until smooth. Stir the chocolate into the chestnut mixture until combined, then add the brandy.

3 Pour the filling into the cold pastry shell, spreading evenly. Chill until set. Decorate with whipped cream and chocolate leaves, if desired, or simply add a dusting of sifted cocoa.

3 To make the filling, mix the egg yolks, cornstarch and 2 tablespoons of the sugar in a bowl. Heat the milk in a saucepan until almost boiling, then beat into the egg mixture. Return to the clean pan and stir over low heat until the custard has thickened and is smooth. Pour half the custard into a bowl.

4 Put the chocolate in a heatproof bowl. Place over a saucepan of barely simmering water until the chocolate has melted, stirring occasionally, until smooth. Stir the melted chocolate into the custard in the bowl, with the vanilla. Spread the filling in the pastry shell and cover closely with dampened wax paper or plastic wrap to prevent the formation of a skin. Let cool, then chill until set.

5 Sprinkle the gelatin over the water in a bowl, leave until spongy, then place the bowl over a pan of simmering water until all the gelatin has dissolved. Stir into the remaining custard, then add the rum.

6 Whisk the egg whites in a clean, grease-free bowl until peaks form. Whisk in the remaining sugar, a little at a time, until stiff, then fold the egg whites quickly but evenly into the rum-flavored custard.

7 Spoon the rum-flavored custard over the chocolate layer in the pastry shell. Using a spatula, level the mixture, making sure that none of the chocolate custard is visible. Return the pie to the refrigerator until the top layer has set, then remove the pie from the pan and place it on a serving plate. Whip the cream, spread it over the pie and sprinkle with chocolate curls, to decorate.

LUXURY WHITE CHOCOLATE CHEESECAKE

SERVES 16–20

5 ounces (about 16–18) graham crackers
½ cup blanched hazelnuts, toasted
¼ cup unsalted butter, melted
½ teaspoon ground cinnamon
white chocolate curls, to decorate
cocoa powder, for dusting (optional)

FOR THE FILLING

12 ounces white chocolate, chopped into small pieces
½ cup heavy cream
3 x 8-ounce packages cream cheese, softened
¼ cup sugar
4 eggs
2 tablespoons hazelnut-flavored liqueur or 1 tablespoon vanilla extract

FOR THE TOPPING

1¾ cups sour cream
¼ cup sugar
1 tablespoon hazelnut-flavored liqueur or 1 teaspoon vanilla extract

3 Using a hand-held electric mixer, beat the cream cheese and sugar in a large bowl until smooth. Add the eggs one at a time, beating well. Slowly beat in the white chocolate mixture and liqueur. Pour the filling into the baked crust. Place the pan on the hot baking sheet. Bake for 45–55 minutes, and do not let the top brown. Transfer the cheesecake to a wire rack while preparing the topping. Increase the oven temperature to 400°F.

4 Prepare the topping. In a small bowl whisk the sour cream, sugar and liqueur until thoroughly mixed. Pour the mixture over the cheesecake, spreading it evenly, and return to the oven. Bake for 5–7 more minutes. Turn off the oven, but do not open the door for one hour. Serve the cheesecake at room temperature, decorated with the white chocolate curls. Dust the surface lightly with cocoa powder, if desired.

1 Preheat oven to 350°F. Grease a 9-inch springform pan. In a food processor, process the graham crackers and hazelnuts until fine crumbs form. Pour in the butter and cinnamon. Process just until blended. Using the back of a spoon, press onto the base and to within ½ inch of the top of the cake pan. Bake the crumb crust for 5–7 minutes, until just set. Cool in the pan on a wire rack. Lower the oven temperature to 300°F and place a baking sheet inside to heat up.

2 To prepare the filling, in a small saucepan over a low heat, melt the white chocolate and cream until smooth, stirring frequently. Set aside to cool slightly.

CHOCOLATE TIRAMISU TART

SERVES 12–16

½ cup unsalted butter

1 tablespoon coffee-flavored liqueur or water

1½ cups all-purpose flour

¼ cup cocoa powder

¼ cup confectioners' sugar

pinch of salt

½ teaspoon vanilla extract

cocoa powder, for dusting

FOR THE CHOCOLATE LAYER

1½ cups heavy cream

1 tablespoon corn syrup

4 ounces bittersweet chocolate, chopped into small pieces

2 tablespoons unsalted butter, cut into small pieces

2 tablespoons coffee-flavored liqueur

FOR THE FILLING

1 cup heavy cream

1½ cups mascarpone cheese, at room temperature

3 tablespoons confectioners' sugar

3 tablespoons cold espresso or strong black coffee

3 tablespoons coffee-flavored liqueur

3½ ounces unsweetened chocolate, grated

1 Make the pastry. Lightly grease a 9-inch springform pan. In a saucepan, heat the butter and liqueur until the butter has melted. Sift the flour, cocoa, confectioners' sugar and salt into a bowl. Remove the butter mixture from the heat, stir in the vanilla and gradually stir into the flour mixture until a soft dough forms.

2 Knead lightly until smooth. Press onto the base and up the sides of the pan to within ¾ inch of the top. Prick the dough. Chill for 40 minutes. Preheat oven to 375°F. Bake the pastry shell for 8–10 minutes. If the pastry puffs up, prick it with a fork and bake for 2–3 more minutes until set. Cool in the pan on a rack.

3 To prepare the chocolate layer, bring the cream and syrup to a boil in a pan over medium heat. Off the heat, add the chocolate, stirring until melted. Beat in the butter and liqueur and pour into the pastry case. Cool completely, then chill.

4 Prepare the filling. Using a hand-held electric mixer, whip the cream in a bowl until soft peaks form. In another bowl, beat the cheese until soft, then beat in the confectioners' sugar until smooth and creamy. Gradually beat in the cold coffee and liqueur; gently fold in the cream and chocolate. Spoon the filling into the pastry shell on top of the chocolate layer. Spread evenly. Chill until ready to serve.

5 To serve, run a sharp knife around the side of the pan to loosen the tart shell. Remove the side of the pan and slide the tart onto a plate. Sift a layer of cocoa powder over the tart to decorate, or pipe rosettes of whipped cream around the rim and top each with a chocolate-coated coffee bean. Chocolate Tiramisu Tart is very rich, so serve it in small wedges, with cups of espresso.

RASPBERRY, MASCARPONE AND WHITE CHOCOLATE CHEESECAKE

SERVES 8

¼ cup unsalted butter

8 ounces ginger cookies, crushed

½ cup chopped pecans or walnuts

FOR THE FILLING

1¼ cups mascarpone cheese

¾ cup ricotta cheese

2 eggs, beaten

3 tablespoons sugar

9 ounces white chocolate, chopped into small pieces

1½ cups fresh or frozen raspberries

FOR THE TOPPING

½ cup mascarpone cheese

⅓ cup ricotta cheese

white chocolate curls and fresh raspberries, to decorate

1 Preheat oven to 300°F. Melt the butter in a saucepan, then stir in the crushed cookies and nuts. Press into the base of a 9-inch springform cake pan. Spread evenly.

2 To make the filling, using a wooden spoon, beat the mascarpone and ricotta in a large mixing bowl, then beat in the eggs, a little at a time. Add the sugar. Beat until the sugar has dissolved, and the mixture is smooth and creamy.

3 Melt the white chocolate gently in a heatproof bowl over a saucepan of simmering water, then stir into the cheese mixture. Add the fresh or frozen raspberries and mix lightly.

4 Pour into the prepared pan and spread evenly, then bake for about one hour or until just set. Switch off the oven, but do not remove the cheesecake. Let cool until completely set.

5 Remove the sides of the pan and carefully lift the cheesecake onto a serving plate. Make the topping by mixing the mascarpone and ricotta cheese in a bowl and spreading the mixture over the cheesecake. Decorate with chocolate curls and raspberries.

APRICOT AND WHITE CHOCOLATE CHEESECAKE

Use 1 cup dried apricots instead of the fresh or frozen raspberries in the cheesecake mixture. Cut the apricots into thin slices or dice them. Omit the mascarpone and ricotta cheese topping and serve the cheesecake with an apricot sauce, made by poaching 8 ounces pitted fresh apricots in ½ cup water until tender, then rubbing the fruit and liquid through a sieve placed over a bowl. Sweeten the apricot purée with sugar to taste, and add enough lemon juice to sharpen the flavor. Alternatively, purée drained canned apricots with a little of their syrup, then stir in lemon juice to taste.

MISSISSIPPI MUD PIE

SERVES 8

1½ cups all-purpose flour

½ teaspoon salt

½ cup butter

2–3 tablespoons ice water

FOR THE FILLING

3 ounces plain chocolate, broken into
small pieces

¼ cup butter or margarine

3 tablespoons corn syrup

3 eggs, beaten

⅔ cup light brown sugar

1 teaspoon vanilla extract

TO DECORATE

4 ounces chocolate bar

1¼ cups heavy cream

1 Preheat oven to 425°F. Sift the flour and salt into a mixing bowl. Rub in the butter until the mixture resembles coarse bread crumbs. Sprinkle in the water, about 1 tablespoon at a time, and toss the mixture lightly with your fingers or a fork until the dough forms a ball.

2 On a lightly floured surface, roll out the pastry and line a 9-inch tart pan, easing in the pastry and being careful not to stretch it. With your thumbs, make a fluted edge.

3 Using a fork, prick the base and sides of the pastry case. Bake for 10–15 minutes, until lightly browned. Cool in the pan on a wire rack.

4 Make the filling. In a heatproof bowl set over a pan of barely simmering water, melt the chocolate with the butter and the corn syrup. Remove the bowl from the heat and stir in the eggs, sugar and vanilla.

5 Lower the oven temperature to 350°F. Pour the chocolate mixture into the pastry shell. Bake for 35–40 minutes, until the filling is set. Let cool completely in the tart pan, on a rack.

6 Make the decoration. Use the heat of your hands to soften the chocolate bar slightly. Working over a sheet of baking parchment, draw the blade of a swivel-bladed vegetable peeler across the side of the chocolate bar to shave off short, wide curls. Chill the curls until needed.

7 Before serving the pie, pour the cream into a bowl and whip to soft peaks. Spread over the top of the pie, hiding the chocolate filling completely. Decorate with the chocolate curls.

ITALIAN CHOCOLATE RICOTTA PIE

SERVES 6

2 cups all-purpose flour
2 tablespoons cocoa powder
¼ cup sugar
½ cup unsalted butter
¼ cup dry sherry
FOR THE FILLING
2 egg yolks
½ cup sugar
2½ cups ricotta cheese
finely grated zest of 1 lemon
6 tablespoons chocolate chips
5 tablespoons chopped candied peel
3 tablespoons chopped angelica

1 Sift the flour and cocoa into a bowl, then stir in the sugar. Rub in the butter using your fingertips, then work in the sherry to make a firm dough.

2 Preheat oven to 400°F. Roll out three-quarters of the pastry on a lightly floured surface and line a 9-inch flan pan with a removable base.

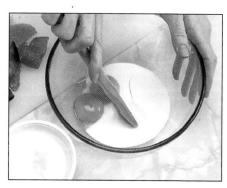

3 Make the filling. Beat the egg yolks and sugar in a bowl, then beat in the ricotta to mix thoroughly. Stir in the lemon zest, chocolate chips, candied peel and angelica.

4 Scrape the ricotta mixture into the pastry shell and spread evenly. Roll out the remaining pastry and cut into strips. Arrange these in a lattice over the pie.

5 Bake for 15 minutes. Lower the oven temperature to 350°F and cook for 30–35 more minutes, until golden brown and firm. Cool the pie in the pan. Serve at room temperature.

White Chocolate and Mango Cream Tart

Serves 8

1½ cups all-purpose flour

1 cup sweetened, dry shredded coconut

½ cup butter, softened

2 tablespoons sugar

2 egg yolks

½ teaspoon almond extract

2½ cups heavy cream

1 large ripe mango

½ cup toasted slivered almonds, to decorate

For the White Chocolate Custard Filling

5 ounces white chocolate, chopped into small pieces

½ cup heavy cream

5 tablespoons cornstarch

1 tablespoons all-purpose flour

¼ cup sugar

1½ cups milk

5 egg yolks

1 Using a hand-held electric mixer at low speed, beat the flour, coconut, butter, sugar, egg yolks and almond extract in a deep bowl until the mixture forms a soft dough. Lightly grease a 9-inch tart pan with a removable base. Press the pastry onto the bottom and sides. Prick the pastry shell with a fork. Chill the shell for 30 minutes.

Cook's Tip

Choose a mango that is a rich yellow in color, with a pink or red blush. It should just yield to the touch, but should not be too soft. Peel it carefully, then cut it in half around the pit. Cut each piece in half again, then slice.

2 Preheat oven to 350°F. Line the pastry shell with baking parchment; fill with baking stones and bake blind for 10 minutes. Remove the paper and stones and bake for 5–7 more minutes, until golden. Cool the cooked pastry in the pan on a wire rack.

3 Prepare the custard filling. In a small saucepan over low heat, melt the white chocolate with the cream, stirring until smooth. Set aside. Combine the cornstarch, flour and sugar in a medium saucepan. Stir in the milk gradually. Place over medium heat and cook, stirring constantly, until the mixture has thickened.

4 Beat the egg yolks in a small bowl. Slowly add about 1 cup of the hot milk mixture, stirring constantly. Return the yolk mixture to the rest of the sauce in the pan, stirring constantly.

5 Bring the custard filling to a gentle boil, stirring constantly until thickened. Stir in the melted white chocolate until well blended. Cool to room temperature, stirring frequently to prevent a skin from forming on the surface. Beat the cream in a medium-sized bowl until soft peaks form. Fold approximately ½ cup of the cream into the white chocolate custard and spoon half the custard into the base. Peel the mango and slice thinly into pieces.

6 With the aid of a metal spatula, arrange the mango slices over the custard in concentric circles, starting at the rim and then filling in the center. Carefully pour the remaining custard over the mango slices, spreading evenly. Remove the side of the pan and slide the tart carefully onto a serving plate.

7 Spoon the remaining flavored cream into a large piping bag fitted with a medium star tip. Pipe the cream in a scroll pattern in parallel rows on top of the tart, keeping the rows about ½ inch apart. Carefully sprinkle the toasted almonds between the rows. Serve the tart chilled.

HAZELNUT CHOCOLATE MERINGUE TORTE WITH PEARS

SERVES 8–10

¾ cup sugar

1 vanilla bean, split

2 cups water

4 ripe pears, peeled, halved and cored

2 tablespoons hazelnut- or pear-flavored
liqueur

1¼ cups hazelnuts, toasted

6 egg whites

pinch of salt

2¼ cups confectioners' sugar

1 teaspoon vanilla extract

2 ounces unsweetened chocolate, melted

FOR THE CHOCOLATE CREAM

10 ounces bittersweet or unsweetened
chocolate, chopped into small pieces

2 cups heavy cream

¼ cup hazelnut- or pear-flavored liqueur

1 In a saucepan large enough to hold the pears in a single layer combine the sugar, vanilla bean and water. Over high heat, bring to a boil, stirring until the sugar dissolves. Lower the heat, add the pears to the syrup, cover and simmer gently for 12–15 minutes, until tender. Remove the pan from the heat and let the pears cool in their poaching liquid. Carefully lift the pears out of the liquid and drain on paper towels. Transfer them to a plate, sprinkle with liqueur, cover and chill overnight.

2 Preheat oven to 350°F. With a pencil draw a 9-inch circle on each of two sheets of baking parchment. Turn the paper over onto two baking sheets (so the pencil marks are underneath). Pulse the toasted hazelnuts in a food processor fitted with a metal blade.

3 In a large bowl, beat the whites with a hand-held electric mixer until frothy. Add the salt and beat on high speed until soft peaks form. Reduce the mixer speed and gradually add the confectioners' sugar, beating well after each addition until all the sugar has been added and the whites are stiff and glossy; this will take 12–15 minutes. Gently fold in the nuts and vanilla and spoon the meringue onto the circles on the baking sheets, smoothing the top and sides.

4 Bake for one hour until the tops are dry and firm. Turn off the oven and allow to cool in the oven for 2–3 hours or overnight, until completely dry.

5 Prepare the chocolate cream. Melt the chocolate in a heatproof bowl set over a saucepan of simmering water. Stir the chocolate until melted and smooth. Cool to room temperature. Using a hand-held electric mixer beat the cream in a bowl to form soft peaks. Quickly fold the cream into the melted chocolate; fold in the liqueur. Spoon about one third of the chocolate cream into an icing bag fitted with a star tip. Set aside.

6 Cut each pear half into thin slices with a sharp knife. Place one meringue layer on a serving plate. Spread with half the chocolate cream and arrange half the sliced pears evenly over the cream. Pipe a border of rosettes around the edge.

7 Top with the second meringue layer and spread with the remaining chocolate cream. Arrange the remaining pear slices in an attractive pattern over the chocolate cream. Pipe a border of rosettes around the edge. Spoon the melted chocolate into a small paper cone and drizzle the chocolate over the pears. Chill for at least one hour before serving.

CHOCOLATE, BANANA AND TOFFEE PIE

SERVES 6

5 tablespoons unsalted butter, melted
9 ounces milk chocolate graham crackers
crushed
chocolate curls, to decorate

FOR THE FILLING

1 can (13 ounces) condensed milk
5 ounces unsweetened chocolate, chopped
½ cup crème fraîche
1 tablespoon corn syrup

FOR THE TOPPING

2 bananas
1 cup crème fraîche
2 teaspoons strong black coffee

1 Mix the butter with the cookie crumbs. Press onto the base and sides of a 9-inch loose-based tart pan. Chill.

2 Make the filling. Place the unopened can of condensed milk in a deep saucepan of boiling water, making sure that it is completely covered. Lower the heat and simmer, covered for 2 hours, adding water as necessary. The can must remain covered at all times.

3 Remove the pan from the heat and set aside, covered, until the can has cooled down completely in the water. Do not attempt to open the can until it is completely cold.

4 Gently melt the chocolate with the crème fraîche and golden corn in a heatproof bowl over a saucepan of simmering water. Stir in the caramelized condensed milk and beat until evenly mixed. Pour the filling into the cookie crust and spread it evenly.

5 Slice the bananas evenly and arrange them over the chocolate filling.

6 Stir the crème fraîche and coffee together in a bowl, then spoon the mixture over the bananas. Sprinkle the chocolate curls on top. Or, omit the crème fraîche topping and decorate with whipped cream and extra banana slices.

COLD DESSERTS

CHOCOLATE PROFITEROLES

4 Beat 1 egg in a small bowl and set aside. Add the whole eggs, one at a time, to the flour mixture, beating well after each addition. Beat in just enough of the beaten egg to make a smooth, shiny dough. It should pull away and fall slowly when dropped from a spoon.

5 Using a tablespoon, ease the dough in 12 mounds onto the prepared baking sheet. Bake for 25–30 minutes, until the puffs are golden brown.

6 Remove the puffs from the oven and cut a small slit in the side of each of them to release the steam. Return the puffs to the oven, turn off the heat and let them dry out, with the oven door open.

7 Remove the ice cream from the freezer and let it soften for about 10 minutes. Split the profiteroles in half and put a small scoop of ice cream in each. Arrange on a serving platter or divide among individual plates. Pour the sauce over the profiteroles and serve immediately.

VARIATION

Fill the profiteroles with whipped cream, if you prefer. Spoon the cream into a piping bag and fill the slit puffs, or sandwich the halved puffs with the cream.

SERVES 4-6

1 cup all-purpose flour
¼ teaspoon salt
pinch of freshly grated nutmeg
¾ cup water
6 tablespoons unsalted butter, cut into
6 equal pieces
3 eggs
3 cups vanilla ice cream

FOR THE CHOCOLATE SAUCE

10 ounces unsweetened chocolate, chopped into small pieces
½ cup warm water

1 Preheat oven to 400°F. Grease a baking sheet. Sift the flour, salt and nutmeg onto a sheet of wax paper or foil.

2 To make the sauce, melt the chocolate with the water in a heatproof bowl placed over a saucepan of barely simmering water. Stir until smooth. Keep warm until ready to serve, or reheat when required.

3 In a medium saucepan, bring the water and butter to a boil. Remove from the heat and add the dry ingredients all at once, funneling them in from the paper or foil. Beat with a wooden spoon for about 1 minute, until well blended and the mixture starts to pull away from the pan, then set the pan over low heat and cook the mixture for about 2 minutes, beating constantly. Remove from the heat.

CHOCOLATE CONES WITH APRICOT SAUCE

SERVES 6

9 ounces dark chocolate, chopped into small
pieces
1½ cups ricotta cheese
3 tablespoons heavy cream
2 tablespoons brandy
2 tablespoons confectioners' sugar
finely grated zest of 1 lemon
pared strips of lemon zest, to decorate

FOR THE SAUCE
⅔ cup apricot jam
3 tablespoons lemon juice

1 Cut twelve 4-inch double thickness rounds from baking parchment and shape each into a cone. Secure with masking tape.

2 Melt the chocolate over a saucepan of simmering water. Cool slightly, then spoon a little into each cone, swirling and brushing it to coat the paper evenly.

3 Support each cone point downward in a cup or glass held on its side, to keep it level. Leave in a cool place until the cones are completely set. Unless it is a very hot day, do not put the cones in the refrigerator, as this may mar their appearance.

4 To make the sauce, combine the apricot jam and lemon juice in a small saucepan. Melt over gentle heat, stirring occasionally, then press through a sieve into a small bowl. Set aside to cool.

5 Beat the ricotta cheese in a bowl until softened, then beat in the cream, brandy and confectioners' sugar. Stir in the lemon zest. Spoon the mixture into a piping bag. Fill the cones, then carefully peel off the baking parchment.

6 Spoon a pool of apricot sauce onto six dessert plates. Arrange the cones in pairs on the plates. Sprinkle with pared lemon zest strips and serve immediately.

CHOCOLATE HAZELNUT GALETTES

SERVES 4

6 ounces unsweetened chocolate, chopped into small pieces

3 tablespoons light cream

2 tablespoons slivered hazelnuts

4 ounces white chocolate, chopped into small pieces

¾ cup ricotta cheese

1 tablespoon dry sherry

¼ cup finely chopped hazelnuts, toasted gooseberries, dipped in white chocolate, to decorate

1 Melt the plain chocolate in a heatproof bowl over a saucepan of barely simmering water, then remove the pan from the heat and lift off the bowl. Stir the cream into the melted chocolate. Draw twelve 3-inch circles on sheets of baking parchment.

2 Turn the baking paper over and spread the chocolate over each marked circle, covering in a thin, even layer. Scatter hazelnuts over four of the circles, then let set.

3 Melt the white chocolate in a heatproof bowl over hot water, then stir in the ricotta cheese and dry sherry. Fold in the chopped, toasted hazelnuts. Let cool until the mixture holds its shape.

4 Remove the chocolate rounds carefully from the paper and sandwich them together in stacks of three, spooning the white chocolate hazelnut cream between the layers and using the hazelnut-covered rounds on top. Chill before serving.

5 To serve, place the galettes on individual plates and decorate with chocolate-dipped gooseberries.

CHOCOLATE VANILLA TIMBALES

SERVES 6

1½ cups low-fat milk
2 tablespoons cocoa powder
2 eggs
2 teaspoons vanilla extract
3 tablespoons sugar
1 package powdered gelatin
3 tablespoons hot water
extra cocoa powder, to decorate

FOR THE SAUCE
½ cup light plain yogurt
1½ tablespoons vanilla extract

1 Place the milk and cocoa powder in a saucepan and stir until the milk is boiling. Separate the eggs and beat the egg yolks with the vanilla and sugar in a bowl, until the mixture is smooth. Gradually pour in the chocolate milk, beating well.

2 Return the mixture to the pan and stir constantly over gentle heat, without boiling, until it is slightly thickened and smooth.

3 Remove the pan from the heat. Pour the gelatin into the hot water and stir until it is completely dissolved, then quickly stir it into the milk mixture. Put this mixture aside and let it cool until it is almost set.

4 Whisk the egg whites until they hold soft peaks. Fold the egg whites quickly into the milk mixture. Spoon the timbale mixture into six individual molds and chill them until set.

5 To serve, run a knife around the edge, dip the molds quickly into hot water and turn out. Dust with cocoa. For the sauce, stir together the yogurt and vanilla and spoon onto the plates.

TIRAMISU IN CHOCOLATE CUPS

SERVES 6

1 egg yolk
2 tablespoons sugar
½ teaspoon vanilla extract
1 cup mascarpone cheese
½ cup strong black coffee
1 tablespoon cocoa powder
2 tablespoons coffee liqueur
16 Amaretti cookies
cocoa powder, for dusting
FOR THE CHOCOLATE CUPS
6 ounces unsweetened chocolate, chopped
2 tablespoons unsalted butter

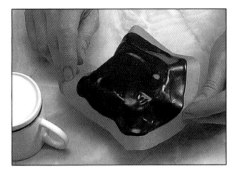

1 Make the chocolate cups. Cut out six 6-inch rounds of baking parchment. Melt the chocolate with the butter in a heatproof bowl over a saucepan of simmering water. Stir until smooth, then spread a spoonful of the chocolate mixture over each circle, to within ¾ inch of the edge.

2 Carefully lift each paper round and drape it over an upturned teacup or ramekin so the edges curve into frills. Let it set completely, then carefully lift off and peel away the paper to reveal the chocolate cups.

3 To make the filling, using a hand-held electric mixer, beat the egg yolk and sugar in a bowl until smooth, then stir in the vanilla. Soften the mascarpone if necessary, then stir it into the egg yolk mixture. Beat until smooth.

4 In a separate bowl, mix the coffee, cocoa and liqueur. Break up the cookies, then stir them into the mixture.

5 Place the chocolate cups on individual plates. Divide half the cookie mixture among them, then spoon on half the mascarpone mixture.

6 Spoon on the remaining cookie mixture (including any extra liquid), top with the rest of the mascarpone mixture and dust lightly with cocoa powder. Chill for about 30 minutes before serving.

White Chocolate Parfait

Serves 10

8 ounces white chocolate, chopped into
small pieces
2½ cups heavy cream
½ cup milk
10 egg yolks
1 tablespoon sugar
½ cup shredded coconut
½ cup canned sweetened coconut milk
1¼ cups unsalted macadamia nuts
curls of fresh coconut, to decorate
For the Chocolate Icing

8 ounces unsweetened chocolate, chopped into
small pieces
6 tablespoons butter
1 tablespoon corn syrup
¾ cup heavy cream

1 Carefully line the base and sides of a 6-cup terrine mold or loaf pan with plastic wrap.

2 Melt the chopped white chocolate with ¼ cup of the cream in the top of a double boiler or a heatproof bowl set over a saucepan of simmering water. Stir continually until the mixture is smooth. Set aside.

3 Put the milk in a pan. Add 1 cup of the remaining cream and bring to a boil over medium heat, stirring constantly.

4 Meanwhile, whisk the egg yolks and sugar together in a large bowl, until thick.

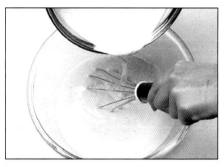

5 Add the hot cream mixture to the yolks, whisking constantly. Pour back into the saucepan and cook over low heat for 2–3 minutes, until thickened. Stir constantly and do not boil. Remove the pan from the heat.

6 Add the melted chocolate, coconut and coconut milk, then stir well and let cool. Whip the remaining cream in a bowl until thick, then fold into the chocolate and coconut mixture.

7 Put 2 cups of the parfait mixture in the prepared mold or pan and spread evenly. Cover and freeze for about 2 hours, until just firm. Cover the remaining mixture and chill.

Variation

White Chocolate and Ginger Parfait: Use sliced preserved ginger instead of macadamia nuts for the central layer of the parfait, and substitute syrup from the jar of ginger for the corn syrup in the icing. Leave out the coconut, if you prefer, and use sweetened condensed milk instead of the coconut milk.

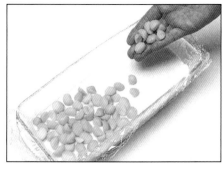

8 Sprinkle the macadamia nuts over the frozen parfait. Spoon in the remaining parfait mixture and smooth evenly. Cover the terrine and freeze for 6–8 hours or overnight, until the parfait is firm.

9 To make the icing, melt the chocolate with the butter and syrup in the top of a double boiler set over hot water. Stir occasionally.

10 Heat the cream in a saucepan, until just simmering, then stir into the chocolate mixture. Remove the pan from the heat and let the mixture cool until lukewarm.

11 To turn out the parfait, wrap the terrine or pan in a hot towel and set it upside down on a plate. Lift off the terrine or pan, then peel off the plastic wrap. Place the parfait on a rack over a baking sheet and pour the icing evenly over the top. Working quickly, smooth the icing down the sides with a spatula. Let set slightly, then transfer to a freezer-proof plate and freeze for 3–4 more hours.

12 Remove from the freezer about 15 minutes before serving, to let the ice cream soften slightly. When ready to serve, cut into slices, using a knife dipped in hot water between each slice. Serve, decorated with coconut curls.

CHOCOLATE AND CHESTNUT POTS

SERVES 6

9 ounces unsweetened chocolate
¼ cup Madeira
2 tablespoons butter, diced
2 eggs, separated
1 cup unsweetened chestnut purée
crème fraîche and chocolate curls, to decorate

1 Make a few chocolate curls for decoration, then break the rest of the chocolate into squares and melt it with the Madeira in a heatproof bowl over a saucepan of barely simmering water. Remove from the heat and add the butter, a few pieces at a time, stirring until melted and smooth.

2 Beat the egg yolks quickly into the mixture, then beat in the chestnut purée, a little at a time, making sure that each addition is absorbed before you add the next, mixing until smooth.

3 Whisk the egg whites in a clean, grease-free bowl until stiff. Stir about 1 tablespoon of the whites into the chestnut mixture to lighten it, then fold in the rest evenly.

4 Spoon the mixture into six small ramekins or custard cups and chill until set. Serve the pots topped with a generous spoonful of crème fraîche or whipped cream. Decorate with the chocolate curls.

MOCHA VELVET CREAM POTS

SERVES 8

1 tablespoon instant coffee powder
2 cups milk
6 tablespoons sugar
8 ounces unsweetened chocolate, chopped into small pieces
2 teaspoons vanilla extract
2 tablespoons coffee liqueur (optional)
7 egg yolks
whipped cream, to decorate

1 Preheat oven to 325°F. Place eight ½-cup custard cups or ramekins in a roasting pan. Set the pan aside.

2 Put the instant coffee into a saucepan. Stir in the milk, then add the sugar and set the pan over medium heat. Bring to a boil, stirring constantly, until both the coffee and the sugar have dissolved completely.

3 Remove the pan from the heat and add the chocolate. Stir until it has melted and the sauce is smooth. Stir in the vanilla and coffee liqueur, if using.

4 In a bowl, whisk the egg yolks to blend them lightly. Slowly whisk in the chocolate mixture until well mixed, then strain the mixture into a large pitcher and divide equally among the cups or ramekins. Pour enough boiling water into the roasting pan to come halfway up the sides of the cups or ramekins. Carefully place the roasting pan in the oven.

5 Bake for 30–35 minutes, until the custard is just set and a knife inserted into the custard comes out clean. Remove the cups or ramekins from the roasting pan and let cool. Place on a baking sheet, cover and chill completely. Decorate with whipped cream, if desired.

CHOCOLATE PAVLOVA WITH PASSION FRUIT CREAM

SERVES 6

4 egg whites

1 cup sugar

4 teaspoons cornstarch

3 tablespoons cocoa powder

1 teaspoon vinegar

chocolate leaves, to decorate

FOR THE FILLING

5 ounces unsweetened chocolate, chopped into small pieces

1 cup heavy cream

⅔ cup plain yogurt

½ teaspoon vanilla extract

4 passion fruit

1 Preheat oven to 275°F. Cut a piece of baking parchment to fit a baking sheet. Draw a 9-inch circle on the paper.

2 Whisk the egg whites in a clean, grease-free bowl until stiff. Gradually whisk in the sugar and continue to whisk until the mixture is stiff again. Whisk in the cornstarch, cocoa and vinegar.

3 Place the baking parchment upside down on the baking sheet. Spread the mixture over the marked circle, making a slight dip in the center. Bake for 1½–2 hours.

4 To make the filling, melt the chocolate in a heatproof bowl over barely simmering water, then remove from the heat and cool slightly. In a separate bowl, whip the cream with the yogurt and vanilla until thick. Fold ¼ cup into the chocolate, then set both mixtures aside.

5 Halve all the passion fruit and scoop out the pulp. Stir half into the cream mixture. Carefully remove the meringue shell from the baking sheet and place it on a large serving plate. Fill with the passion fruit cream, then spoon on the chocolate mixture and the remaining passion fruit pulp.

6 Decorate with chocolate leaves and serve as soon as possible, while the meringue is still crisp on the outside and chewy within.

Chocolate Sorbet

Serves 6

5 ounces bittersweet chocolate, chopped
4 ounces unsweetened chocolate, grated
1¼ cups sugar
2 cups water
chocolate curls, to decorate

1 Put all the chocolate in a food processor, fitted with the metal blade, and process for 20–30 seconds, until finely chopped.
2 In a saucepan over a medium heat, bring the sugar and water to a boil, stirring until the sugar dissolves. Boil for about 2 minutes, then remove the pan from the heat.
3 With the machine running, pour the hot syrup over the chocolate in the food processor. Keep the machine running for 1–2 minutes until the chocolate is completely melted and the mixture is smooth, scraping down the bowl once.
4 Strain the chocolate mixture into a large measuring cup or bowl. Let cool, then chill, stirring occasionally. Freeze the mixture in an ice-cream maker. Or, pour into a container suitable for use in the freezer, freeze until slushy, whisk until smooth, then freeze again. Whisk for a second time before the mixture hardens completely. Let the sorbet soften for 5–10 minutes at room temperature and serve in scoops, decorated with chocolate curls.

Chocolate Sorbet with Red Fruit

Serves 6

2 cups water
3 tablespoons honey
½ cup sugar
¾ cup cocoa powder
2 ounces dark or bittersweet chocolate, chopped into small pieces
14 ounces soft red fruits, such as raspberries, red currants or strawberries

1 Place the water, honey, sugar and cocoa powder in a saucepan. Heat gently, stirring occasionally, until the sugar has completely dissolved.
2 Remove the pan from the heat, add the chocolate and stir until melted. Let cool.
3 Pour into an ice-cream maker and churn until frozen. Or, pour into a container suitable for use in the freezer, freeze until slushy, whisk until smooth, then freeze again. Whisk for a second time before the mixture hardens completely, and cover the container.
4 Remove from the freezer 10–15 minutes before serving, so the sorbet softens slightly. Serve in scoops in chilled dessert bowls, with the fruit.

CHOCOLATE MINT ICE CREAM PIE

SERVES 8

3 ounces chocolate chips
1½ ounces butter or margarine
2 ounces crispy rice cereal
4 cups mint-chocolate-chip ice cream
chocolate curls, to decorate

1 Line a 9-inch pie pan with foil. Place a round of wax paper over the foil in the bottom of the pan.

2 In a heatproof bowl set over a saucepan of simmering water melt the chocolate chips with the butter or margarine.

3 Remove the bowl from the heat and gently stir in the cereal, a little at a time.

4 Press the chocolate-cereal mixture evenly over the base and up the sides of the prepared pan, forming a ½-inch rim. Chill until completely hard.

5 Carefully remove the cereal crust from the pan and peel off the foil and paper. Return the base to the pie pan.

6 Remove the ice cream from the freezer and let it soften for 10 minutes.

7 Spread the ice cream evenly in the cereal crust. Freeze until firm.

8 Sprinkle the chocolate curls over the ice cream just before serving.

ICE CREAM BOMBES

SERVES 6

4 cups softened chocolate ice cream
*2 cups softened vanilla
ice cream*
⅓ cup chocolate chips
4 ounces toffee candies
5 tablespoons heavy cream

1 Divide the chocolate ice cream equally among six small cups. Spread it to the base and up the sides, leaving a small cup-shaped dip in the middle. Return to the freezer and let sit for 45 minutes. Take the cups out again and smooth the ice cream in each into shape, keeping the center hollow. Return to the freezer.

2 Put the vanilla ice cream in a small bowl and break it up slightly with a spoon. Stir in the chocolate chips and use this mixture to fill the hollows in the cups of chocolate ice cream. Smooth the tops, then cover the cups with plastic wrap, return to the freezer and leave overnight.

3 Melt the toffee candies with the cream in a small pan over a very low heat, stirring constantly until smooth, warm and creamy.
4 Turn out the bombes onto individual plates and pour the toffee sauce over the top. Serve immediately.

CHOCOLATE FUDGE SUNDAES

SERVES 4

4 scoops each vanilla and coffee ice cream
2 small ripe bananas
whipped cream
toasted slivered almonds
FOR THE SAUCE
⅓ cup light brown sugar
½ cup corn syrup
3 tablespoons strong black coffee
1 teaspoon ground cinnamon
5 ounces unsweetened chocolate, chopped into small pieces
5 tablespoons heavy cream
3 tablespoons coffee-flavored liqueur (optional)

1 To make the sauce, place the sugar, syrup, coffee and cinnamon in a heavy saucepan. Bring to a boil, then boil for about 5 minutes, stirring the mixture constantly.

2 Turn off the heat and stir in the chocolate. When the chocolate has melted and the mixture is smooth, stir in the cream and the liqueur, if using. Let the sauce cool slightly. If made ahead, reheat the sauce gently until just warm.

3 Fill four glasses with a scoop each of vanilla and coffee ice cream.

4 Peel the bananas and cut into thin slices. Scatter the sliced bananas over the ice cream. Pour the warm fudge sauce over the bananas, then top each sundae with a generous swirl of whipped cream. Sprinkle the sundaes with toasted almonds and serve immediately.

CHOCOLATE ICE CREAM

SERVES 4–6

3 cups milk
4-inch piece vanilla bean
4 egg yolks
½ cup sugar
8 ounces unsweetened chocolate, chopped into
small pieces

1 Heat the milk with the vanilla bean in a small saucepan. Remove from the heat as soon as small bubbles start to form on the surface. Do not let it boil. Strain the milk into a pitcher and set aside.

2 Using a wire whisk or hand-held electric mixer, beat the egg yolks in a bowl. Gradually whisk in the sugar and continue to whisk until the mixture is thick. Slowly add the milk to the egg mixture, whisking after each addition. When all the milk has been added, pour the mixture into a heatproof bowl.

3 Place the heatproof bowl over a saucepan of simmering water and add the chocolate. Stir over low heat until the chocolate melts, then raise the heat slightly and continue to stir the chocolate-flavored custard until it thickens enough to coat the back of a wooden spoon lightly. Remove the custard from the heat, pour into a bowl and let cool, stirring occasionally to prevent skin from forming on the surface.

4 Freeze the chocolate mixture in an ice-cream maker, following the manufacturer's instructions, or pour it into a suitable container for freezing. Freeze for about 3 hours or until set. Remove from the container and chop into 3-inch pieces. Place in a food processor and chop until smooth. Return to the freezer container and freeze again. Repeat two or three times, until the ice cream is smooth and creamy.

ROCKY ROAD ICE CREAM

SERVES 6

4 ounces unsweetened chocolate, chopped into
small pieces
⅔ cup milk
1¼ cups heavy cream
2 cups marshmallows, chopped
½ cup candied cherries, chopped
½ cup crumbled shortbread cookies
2 tablespoons chopped walnuts

1 Melt the chocolate in the milk in a saucepan over a gentle heat, stirring occasionally. Pour into a bowl and let cool completely.

2 Whip the cream in a separate bowl until it just holds its shape. Beat in the chocolate mixture, a little at a time, until the mixture is smooth and creamy.

3 Pour the mixture into an ice-cream maker and, following the manufacturer's instructions, churn until almost frozen. Or, pour into a container suitable for use in the freezer, freeze until ice crystals form around the edges, then whisk with a large hand whisk or hand-held electric mixer until smooth.

4 Stir the marshmallows, cherries, cookies and nuts into the iced mixture, then return to the freezer container and freeze until firm.

5 Let the ice cream soften at room temperature for 15–20 minutes before serving in scoops. Add a wafer and chocolate sauce to each portion, if desired.

LITTLE CAKES,
COOKIES & BARS

CHUNKY CHOCOLATE BARS

MAKES 12

12 ounces unsweetened chocolate, chopped into
small pieces
½ cup unsalted butter
1 can (14 ounces) condensed milk
8 ounces graham crackers, broken
⅓ cup raisins
4 ounces pitted dried peaches, coarsely chopped
½ cup hazelnuts or pecans, coarsely chopped

1 Line an 11 x 7-inch cake pan with plastic wrap.
2 Melt the chocolate and butter in a large heatproof bowl over a pan of simmering water. Stir until well mixed.

3 Pour the condensed milk into the chocolate and butter mixture. Beat with a wooden spoon until creamy.
4 Add the broken graham crackers, raisins, chopped peaches and hazelnuts. Mix well until all the ingredients are coated in the rich chocolate sauce.

5 Pour the mixture into the prepared pan, making sure it is pressed well into the corners. Leave the top craggy. Cool, then chill until set.
6 Lift out of the pan using the plastic wrap and then peel it off. Cut into 12 bars and serve immediately.

CHOCOLATE LEMON TARTLETS

MAKES 12 TARTLETS
flour, for dusting
1 pound Shortcrust Pastry
lemon twists and melted chocolate to decorate
FOR THE LEMON CUSTARD SAUCE
grated zest and juice of 1 lemon
1½ cups milk
6 egg yolks
½ cup sugar
FOR THE LEMON CURD FILLING
grated zest and juice of 2 lemons
¾ cup unsalted butter, diced
2 cups sugar
3 eggs, lightly beaten
FOR THE CHOCOLATE LAYER
¾ cup heavy cream
6 ounces bittersweet or unsweetened chocolate,
chopped into small pieces
2 tablespoons unsalted butter, cut into pieces

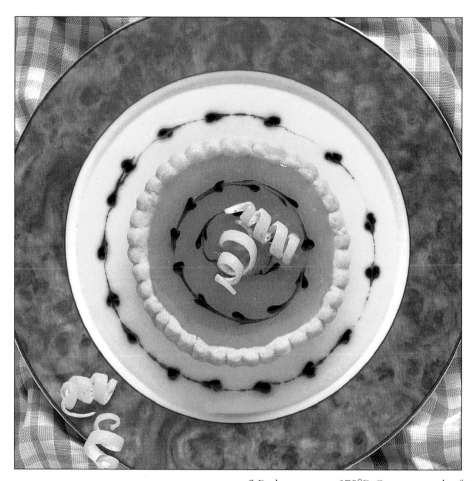

1 To prepare the custard sauce, place the zest in a saucepan with the milk. Bring to a boil over medium heat. Remove from the heat and let stand for 5 minutes to absorb. Strain the milk into a clean pan and reheat it gently.

2 In a bowl beat the yolks and sugar with a hand-held electric mixer for 2–3 minutes, until thick. Add about 1 cup of the flavored hot milk, beating vigorously.

3 Return the yolk mixture to the rest of the milk in the pan and cook gently, stirring constantly over low heat, until the mixture thickens and lightly coats the back of a spoon. (Do not let sauce boil or it will curdle.) Strain into a chilled bowl. Stir 2 tablespoons lemon juice into the sauce. Cool, stirring occasionally, then chill until ready to use.

4 Prepare the lemon curd filling. Combine the lemon zest, juice, butter and sugar in the top of a double boiler. Set over simmering water and heat gently until the butter has melted and the sugar has completely dissolved. Reduce the heat to low.

5 Stir the lightly beaten eggs into the butter mixture. Cook over low heat, for 15 minutes, stirring constantly, until the mixture coats the back of a spoon.

6 Strain the lemon curd into a bowl and cover closely with plastic wrap. Let cool, stirring occasionally, then chill to thicken, stirring occasionally.

7 Lightly butter twelve 3-inch tartlet pans (if possible ones which have removable bases). On a lightly floured surface, roll out the pastry to a thickness of ⅛ inch. Using a 4-inch fluted cutter, cut out 12 rounds and press each one into a tartlet pan. Prick the bases with a fork. Place the pans on a baking sheet and chill for 30 minutes.

8 Preheat oven to 375°F. Cut out rounds of foil and line each pastry shell; fill with baking stones or rice. Bake blind for 5–8 minutes. Remove the foil with the stones and bake for 5 more minutes, until the shells are golden. Cool on rack.

9 Prepare the chocolate layer. In a saucepan over medium heat, bring the cream to a boil. Remove from the heat and add the chocolate all at once; stir until melted. Beat in the butter and cool slightly. Pour the filling into each tartlet to make a layer ¼ inch thick. Chill for 10 minutes, until set.

10 Remove the tartlets from the pans and spoon in a layer of lemon curd to come to the top of the pastry. Set aside, but do not chill. To serve, spoon a little lemon custard sauce onto a plate and place a tartlet in the center. Decorate with a lemon twist. Dot the custard with melted chocolate. Draw a skewer through the chocolate to make heart motifs.

CHOCOLATE-DIPPED HAZELNUT CRESCENTS

MAKES ABOUT 35

2 cups all-purpose flour
pinch of salt
1 cup unsalted butter, softened
6 tablespoons sugar
1 tablespoon hazelnut-flavored liqueur
or water
1 teaspoon vanilla extract
3 ounces unsweetened chocolate, chopped into
small pieces
½ cup hazelnuts, toasted and
finely chopped
confectioners' sugar, for dusting
12 ounces unsweetened chocolate, melted, for
dipping

1 Preheat oven to 325°F. Grease two large baking sheets. Sift the flour and salt into a bowl. In a separate bowl, beat the butter until creamy. Add the sugar and beat until fluffy, then beat in the hazelnut liqueur and the vanilla. Gently stir in the flour mixture, then the chocolate and hazelnuts.

2 With floured hands, shape the dough into 2 x ½-inch crescent shapes. Place on the baking sheets, 2 inches apart. Bake for 20–25 minutes, until the edges are set and the cookies slightly golden. Remove the cookies from the oven and cool on the baking sheets for 10 minutes, then transfer the cookies to wire racks to cool completely.

3 Have the melted chocolate ready in a small bowl. Dust the cookies lightly with confectioners' sugar. Using a pair of kitchen tongs or your fingers, dip half of each crescent into the melted chocolate. Place the crescents on a non-stick baking sheet until the chocolate has set.

BRIOCHES AU CHOCOLAT

MAKES 12

2¼ cups all-purpose flour
pinch of salt
2 tablespoons sugar
1 envelope of dry yeast
3 eggs, beaten, plus extra beaten egg,
for glazing
3 tablespoons room temperature milk
½ cup unsalted butter, diced
6 ounces bittersweet chocolate, broken into
squares

1 Sift the flour and salt into a large mixing bowl and stir in the sugar and yeast. Make a well in the center of the mixture and add the eggs and milk.

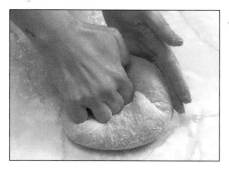

2 Beat the egg and milk mixture well, gradually incorporating the surrounding dry ingredients to make a fairly soft dough. Turn the dough onto a lightly floured surface and knead well for about 5 minutes, until smooth and elastic, adding a little more flour if necessary.
3 Add the butter to the dough, a few pieces at a time, kneading until each addition is absorbed before adding the next. When all the butter has been incorporated and small bubbles appear in the dough, wrap it in plastic wrap and chill for at least 1 hour. If you intend to serve the brioches for breakfast, the dough can be left overnight.

4 Lightly grease 12 individual brioche pans set on a baking sheet or a 12-cup brioche pan. Divide the brioche dough into 12 pieces and shape each into a smooth round. Place a chocolate square in the center of each round. Bring up the sides of the dough and press the edges firmly together to seal. Reserve the remaining chocolate.
5 Place the brioches, seam side down, in the prepared pans. Cover and let them sit in a warm place for about 30 minutes or until doubled in size. Preheat oven to 400°F.

6 Brush the brioches with beaten egg. Bake for 12–15 minutes, until puffed up and golden brown. Place on wire racks and let set until warm. Meanwhile, melt the remaining chocolate in a heatproof bowl placed over a saucepan of simmering water. Drizzle the melted chocolate over the warm brioches and serve.

COOK'S TIP
Brioches freeze well for up to
1 month. Bake the brioches as
suggested, but without the melted
chocolate topping, and freeze. Thaw
at room temperature. Reheat on
baking sheets in a low oven, then
drizzle on the melted chocolate.

CHOCOLATE TOFFEE BARS

MAKES 32

2 cups light brown sugar
2 cups butter or margarine, at room temperature
2 egg yolks
1½ teaspoons vanilla extract
4 cups all-purpose or whole-wheat flour
½ teaspoon salt
6 ounces unsweetened chocolate, broken into squares
1 cup walnuts or pecans, chopped

1 Preheat oven to 350°F. Beat the sugar and butter or margarine in a mixing bowl until light and fluffy. Beat in the egg yolks and vanilla, then stir in the flour and salt to make a soft dough.
2 Spread the dough in a greased 13 x 9 x 2-inch baking pan. Level the surface. Bake for 25–30 minutes, until lightly browned. The texture will be soft.
3 Remove from the oven and immediately place the chocolate squares on the hot base. Set aside until the chocolate softens, then spread it evenly with a spatula. Sprinkle with the chopped nuts.
4 While it is still warm, cut it into 2 x 1½-inch bars, remove from the pan and let cool on a wire rack.

CHOCOLATE PECAN SQUARES

MAKES 16

2 eggs
2 teaspoons vanilla extract
pinch of salt
1½ cups pecans, roughly chopped
½ cup all-purpose flour
¼ cup sugar
½ cup corn syrup
3 ounces unsweetened chocolate, chopped into small pieces
3 tablespoons unsalted butter
16 pecan halves, to decorate

1 Preheat oven to 325°F. Line an 8-inch square baking pan with baking parchment.
2 In a bowl, whisk the eggs with the vanilla and salt. In another bowl, combine the pecans and flour.
3 Put the sugar in a saucepan, add the corn syrup and bring to a boil. Remove from the heat and stir in the chocolate and butter with a wooden spoon until both have dissolved and the mixture is smooth. Stir in the beaten egg mixture, then fold in the pecans and flour.
4 Pour the mixture into the prepared pan and bake for about 35 minutes or until firm to the touch. Cool in the pan for 10 minutes before turning out on a wire rack. Cut into 2-inch squares and press pecan halves into the tops while still warm. Cool completely before serving.

WHITE CHOCOLATE BROWNIES WITH MILK CHOCOLATE MACADAMIA TOPPING

SERVES 12

1 cup all-purpose flour
½ teaspoon baking powder
pinch of salt
6 ounces white chocolate, chopped into small pieces
½ cup sugar
½ cup unsalted butter, cut into small pieces
2 eggs, lightly beaten
1 teaspoon vanilla extract
6 ounces unsweetened chocolate chips or plain chocolate, chopped into small pieces

FOR THE TOPPING

7 ounces milk chocolate, chopped into small pieces
1½ cups unsalted macadamia nuts, chopped

1 Preheat oven to 350°F. Grease a 9-inch springform pan. Sift together the flour, baking powder and salt, set aside.

2 In a medium saucepan over low heat, melt the white chocolate, sugar and butter until smooth, stirring frequently. Cool slightly, then beat in the eggs and vanilla. Stir in the flour mixture until well blended. Stir in the chocolate chips. Spread evenly in the prepared pan.

3 Bake for 20–25 minutes, until a cake tester inserted in the cake pan comes out clean; do not over-bake. Remove the cake from the oven and place the pan on a heatproof surface.

4 Sprinkle the chopped milk chocolate evenly over the brownies and return to the oven for 1 minute.

5 Remove the brownies from the oven again and gently spread the softened chocolate evenly over the top. Sprinkle with the macadamia nuts and gently press them into the chocolate. Cool on a wire rack for 30 minutes, then chill, for about 1 hour, until set. Run a sharp knife around the side of the pan to loosen, then unclip the side of the springform pan and remove it carefully. Cut into thin wedges.

CHUNKY DOUBLE CHOCOLATE COOKIES

MAKES 18–20
½ cup unsalted butter, softened
⅔ cup light brown sugar
1 egg
1 teaspoon vanilla extract
1¼ cups self-rising flour
¾ cup rolled oats
4 ounces unsweetened chocolate, chopped
4 ounces white chocolate, chopped

DOUBLE-CHOC ALMOND COOKIES:
Instead of rolled oats, use ¼ cup ground almonds. Omit the chopped chocolate and use 1 cup chocolate chips instead. Top each mound of cake mixture with half a candied cherry before baking.

<u>1</u> Preheat oven to 375°F. Lightly grease two baking sheets. Cream the butter with the sugar in a bowl until fluffy. Add the egg and vanilla and beat well.
<u>2</u> Sift the flour over the mixture and fold in lightly with a metal spoon, then add the oats and chocolate and stir until evenly mixed.

<u>3</u> Place small spoonfuls of the mixture in 18–20 chunky mounds on the baking sheets, leaving space for spreading.
<u>4</u> Bake for 12–15 minutes or until the cookies are beginning to turn golden. Cool for 2–3 minutes on the baking sheets, then lift onto wire racks. The cookies will be soft when freshly baked but will harden once cooled.

CHOCOLATE KISSES

MAKES 24

3 ounces dark chocolate, chopped into small pieces
3 ounces white chocolate, chopped into small pieces
½ cup butter, softened
½ cup sugar
2 eggs
2 cups all-purpose flour
confectioners' sugar, to decorate

1 Melt the plain and white chocolates in separate bowls and set both aside to cool.
2 Beat the butter and sugar together until fluffy. Beat in the eggs, one at a time. Then sift in the flour and mix well.

3 Halve the creamed mixture and divide it between the two bowls of chocolate. Mix each chocolate in thoroughly so that each forms a dough. Knead the doughs until smooth, wrap them separately in plastic wrap and chill for 1 hour. Preheat oven to 375°F.

4 Shape slightly rounded teaspoonfuls of both doughs into balls. Arrange the balls on greased baking sheets and bake for 10–12 minutes. Dust liberally with sifted confectioners' sugar and cool on a wire rack.

CHOCOLATE CINNAMON TUILES

3 In a separate bowl, combine the cocoa and cinnamon. Stir into the larger quantity of mixture until well combined. Leaving room for spreading, drop spoonfuls of the chocolate-flavored mixture onto the prepared baking sheets, then spread each gently with a sharp knife to make a neat round.

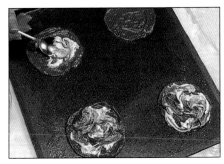

4 Using a small spoon, drizzle the reserved mixture over the rounds, swirling it lightly to give a marbled effect.

5 Bake for 4–6 minutes, until just set. Using a metal spatula, lift each cookie and drape it over a rolling pin, to give a curved shape as it hardens. Allow the tuiles to set, then remove them and finish cooling on a wire rack. Serve on the same day.

MAKES 12

1 egg white
¼ cup sugar
2 tablespoons all-purpose flour
3 tablespoons butter, melted
1 tablespoon cocoa powder
½ teaspoon ground cinnamon

1 Preheat oven to 400°F. Lightly grease two large baking sheets. Whisk the egg white in a clean, grease-free bowl until it forms soft peaks. Gradually whisk in the sugar to make a smooth, glossy mixture.

2 Sift the flour over the meringue mixture and fold in evenly; try not to deflate the mixture. Stir in the butter. Transfer about 3 tablespoons of the mixture to a small bowl and set it aside.

CHOCOLATE CUPS

Cream ⅔ cup butter with ½ cup sugar. Stir in 1 cup rolled oats, 1 tablespoon cocoa powder and 1 teaspoon vanilla extract. Roll to the size of golf balls and space well on greased baking sheets. Bake at 350°F for 12–15 minutes. Cool slightly, then drape over greased upturned glasses until cool and firm.
Makes 8–10.

CHOCOLATE MARZIPAN COOKIES

MAKES ABOUT 36

1 cup unsalted butter, softened

1 cup light brown sugar

1 egg, beaten

2 ¾ cups all-purpose flour

¼ cups cocoa powder

7 ounces white almond paste

4 ounces white chocolate, chopped into small pieces

1 Preheat oven to 375°F. Lightly grease two large baking sheets. Using a hand-held electric mixer, cream the butter with the sugar in a mixing bowl until fluffy. Add the egg and beat well.

2 Sift the flour and cocoa over the mixture. Stir in with a wooden spoon until all the flour mixture has been smoothly incorporated, then use clean hands to press the mixture together to make a fairly soft dough.

3 Using a rolling pin and keeping your touch light, roll out about half the dough on a lightly floured surface to a thickness of about ¼ inch. Using a 2-inch plain or fluted cookie cutter, cut out 36 rounds, re-rolling the dough as required. Wrap the remaining dough in plastic wrap and set it aside.

4 Cut the almond paste into 36 equal pieces. Roll into balls, flatten slightly and place one on each round of dough. Roll out the remaining dough, cut out more rounds, then place on top of the almond paste. Press the dough edges to seal.

5 Bake for 10–12 minutes or until the cookies have puffed up and are beginning to crack on the surface. Cool on the baking sheet for about 2–3 minutes, then finish cooling on a wire rack.

6 Melt the white chocolate, then either drizzle it over the cookies to decorate, or spoon into a paper piping bag and quickly pipe a design onto the cookies.

VARIATION

Use glazed icing instead of melted white chocolate to decorate the cookies, if you prefer.

CANDY & TRUFFLES

DOUBLE CHOCOLATE-DIPPED FRUIT

MAKES 24 COATED PIECES

fruits – about 24 pieces (strawberries, cherries, orange segments, large seedless grapes, gooseberries, kumquats, pitted prunes, pitted dates, dried apricots, dried peaches or dried pears)
4 ounces white chocolate, chopped into small pieces
4 ounces bittersweet chocolate, chopped into small pieces

1 Clean and prepare fruits; wipe strawberries with a soft cloth or brush gently with pastry brush. Wash firm-skinned fruits such as cherries and grapes and dry well. Peel and leave whole or cut up any other fruits being used.

CHOCOLATE PEPPERMINT CREAMS

1 egg white
6 tablespoons heavy cream
1 teaspoon peppermint extract
5½ cups confectioners' sugar, plus extra for dusting
few drops of green food coloring
6 ounces unsweetened chocolate, chopped into small pieces

1 Beat the egg white lightly in a bowl. Mix in the cream and peppermint extract, then gradually add the confectioners' sugar to make a firm, pliable dough. Work in 1–2 drops of green food coloring (apply it from a toothpick to avoid adding too much color) until the dough is an even, pale green.
2 On a surface dusted with confectioners' sugar, roll out the dough to a thickness of about ½ inch. Stamp out 1½-inch rounds and place on a baking sheet lined with baking parchment. Let dry for at least 8 hours, turning once.
3 Melt the chocolate in a bowl over barely simmering water. Let cool slightly. Spread chocolate over the top of each peppermint cream, and place them on fresh sheets of baking parchment. Chill until set.

2 Melt the white chocolate. Remove from the heat and cool to tepid (about 84°F), stirring frequently. Line a baking sheet with baking parchment. Holding each fruit by the stem or end and at an angle, dip about two-thirds of the fruit into the chocolate. Let the excess drip off and place on baking sheet. Chill the fruits for about 20 minutes, until the chocolate sets.

3 Melt the bittersweet chocolate, stirring frequently until smooth.

4 Remove the chocolate from the heat and cool to just below body temperature, about 86°F. Take each white chocolate-coated fruit in turn from the baking sheet and, holding by the stem or end and at the opposite angle, dip the bottom third of each piece into the dark chocolate, creating a chevron effect. Set on the baking sheet. Chill for 15 minutes or until set. Before serving, let the fruit stand at room temperature 10–15 minutes before serving.

RICH CHOCOLATE PISTACHIO FUDGE

MAKES 36

1 cup sugar
1 can (13 ounces) sweetened condensed milk
¼ cup unsalted butter
1 teaspoon vanilla extract
4 ounces dark chocolate, grated
¾ cup pistachios, almonds
or hazelnuts

CHOCOLATE AND MARSHMALLOW FUDGE

2 tablespoons butter
1½ cups sugar
¾ cup evaporated milk
pinch of salt
2 cups white mini marshmallows
1¼ cups chocolate chips
1 teaspoon vanilla extract
½ cup chopped walnuts (optional)

1 Generously grease a 7-inch cake pan. Mix the butter, sugar, evaporated milk and salt in a heavy saucepan. Stir over medium heat until the sugar has dissolved, then bring to a boil and cook for 3–5 minutes or until thickened, stirring constantly.
2 Remove the pan from the heat and beat in the marshmallows and chocolate chips until dissolved. Beat in the vanilla. Scrape the mixture into the prepared cake pan and press it evenly into the corners, using a metal spatula. Level the surface.
3 If using the walnuts, sprinkle them over the fudge and press them into the surface. Set the fudge aside to cool. Before it has set completely, mark it into squares with a sharp knife. Chill until firm before cutting up the fudge and serving it.

1 Grease a 7-inch square cake pan and line with baking parchment. Mix the sugar, condensed milk and butter in a heavy pan. Heat gently, stirring occasionally, until the sugar has dissolved completely and the mixture is smooth.
2 Bring the mixture to a boil, stirring occasionally, and boil until it registers 240°F on a sugar thermometer or until a small amount of the mixture dropped into a cup of ice water forms a soft ball.
3 Remove the pan from the heat and beat in the vanilla, chocolate and nuts. Beat vigorously until the mixture is smooth and creamy.

4 Pour the mixture into the prepared cake pan and spread evenly. Leave until just set, then mark into squares. Let set completely before cutting into squares and removing from the pan. Store in an airtight container in a cool place.

COGNAC AND GINGER CREAMS

MAKES 18–20

*11 ounces unsweetened dark chocolate,
chopped into small pieces
3 tablespoons heavy cream
2 tablespoons cognac
4 pieces preserved ginger, finely chopped
1 tablespoon syrup from the ginger jar
candied ginger, to decorate*

<u>1</u> Polish the insides of 18–20 chocolate molds carefully with cotton. Melt about two-thirds of the chocolate in a heatproof bowl over a saucepan of barely simmering water, then spoon a little into each mold. Reserve a little of the melted chocolate, for sealing the creams.

<u>2</u> Using a small brush, sweep the chocolate up the sides of the molds to coat them evenly, then invert them onto a sheet of wax paper and set aside until the chocolate has set.

CHOCOLATE MARSHMALLOW DIPS

Have ready a large baking sheet lined with baking parchment. Melt 6 ounces bittersweet chocolate in a heatproof bowl over barely simmering water. Stir until smooth. Remove the pan from the heat, but leave the bowl in place, so the chocolate does not solidify too soon. You will need 15–20 large or 30–35 small marshmallows. Using toothpicks, spear each marshmallow and coat in the chocolate. Roll in ground hazelnuts. Place on the lined baking sheet and chill until set before removing the toothpicks. Place each marshmallow dip in a foil candy wrapper.

<u>3</u> Melt the remaining chopped chocolate over simmering water, then stir in the cream, cognac, preserved ginger and ginger syrup, mixing well. Spoon into the chocolate-lined molds. If the reserved chocolate has solidified, melt, then spoon a little into each mold to seal.

<u>4</u> Let the chocolates sit in a cool place (do not refrigerate) until set. To remove them from the molds, gently press them out onto a cool surface, such as a marble slab. Decorate with small pieces of candied ginger. Keep the chocolates cool if not serving them immediately.

CHOCOLATE-COATED NUT BRITTLE

MAKES 20–24 PIECES

1 cup mixed pecans and whole almonds
½ cup sugar
¼ cup water
7 ounces dark chocolate, chopped into small pieces

1 Lightly grease a baking sheet with butter or oil. Mix the nuts, sugar and water in a heavy saucepan. Place the pan over gentle heat, stirring until all the sugar has dissolved.

2 Bring to a boil, then lower the heat to medium and cook until the mixture turns a rich golden brown and registers 310°F on a sugar thermometer. If you do not have a sugar thermometer, test the syrup by adding a few drops to a cup of ice water. The mixture should solidify to a very brittle mass.

CHOCOLATE-COATED HAZELNUTS

Roast about 2 cups hazelnuts in the oven or under the broiler. Let cool. Melt the chocolate in a heatproof bowl over a pan of barely simmering water. Remove from the heat, but leave the bowl over the water so the chocolate remains liquid. Have ready about 30 paper candy wrappers, arranged on baking sheets. Add the roasted hazelnuts to the melted chocolate and stir to coat. Using two spoons, carefully scoop up a cluster of two or three chocolate-coated nuts. Carefully transfer the cluster to a paper candy wrapper. Let the nut clusters set in a cool place.

3 Quickly remove the pan from the heat and pour the mixture onto the prepared baking sheet, spreading it evenly. Let set until completely cold and hard.

4 Break the nut brittle into bite-size pieces. Melt the chocolate and dip the pieces to half-coat them. Let them set on a sheet of baking parchment.

TRUFFLE-FILLED PHYLLO CUPS

MAKES ABOUT 24 CUPS

*3–6 sheets fresh or thawed frozen phyllo
pastry, depending on size*
3 tablespoons unsalted butter, melted
sugar, for sprinkling
pared strips of lemon zest, to decorate
**FOR THE CHOCOLATE TRUFFLE
MIXTURE**
1 cup heavy cream
*8 ounces bittersweet or unsweetened chocolate,
chopped into small pieces*
¼ cup unsalted butter, cut into small pieces
2 tablespoons brandy or liqueur

1 To prepare the truffle mixture, bring
the cream to a boil in a saucepan over a
medium heat. Remove from the heat and
add the pieces of chocolate, stirring until
melted. Beat in the butter and add the
brandy or liqueur. Strain into a bowl and
chill for1 hour, until thick.

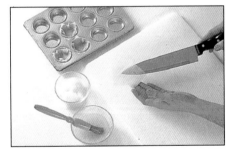

2 Preheat oven to 400°F. Grease a
12-cup cupcake pan. Cut the phyllo
sheets into 2½-inch squares. Cover with a
damp dish towel. Place one square on a
work surface. Brush lightly with melted
butter, turn over and brush the other
side. Sprinkle with a pinch of sugar.
Butter another square and place it over
the first at an angle; sprinkle with sugar.
Butter a third square and place over the
first two, unevenly, so the corners form
an uneven edge. Press the layered square
into one of the cups in the cupcake pan.

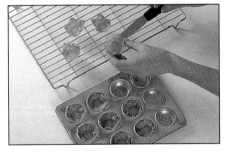

3 Continue to fill the pan, working
quickly so the phyllo does not have time
to dry out. Bake the phyllo cups for 4–6
minutes, until golden. Cool for
10 minutes in the cupcake pan, then
carefully transfer to a wire rack and
cool completely.
4 Stir the chocolate mixture; it should be
just thick enough to pipe. Spoon the
mixture into a piping bag fitted with a
medium star nozzle and pipe a swirl into
each phyllo cup. Decorate each with tiny
strips of lemon zest.

CHOCOLATE TRUFFLES

MAKES 20 LARGE OR 30 MEDIUM TRUFFLES

1 cup heavy cream
10 ounces bittersweet chocolate, chopped into small pieces
3 tablespoons unsalted butter, cut into small pieces
3 tablespoons brandy, whiskey or liqueur of own choice
cocoa powder, for dusting (optional)
finely chopped pistachios, to decorate (optional)
14 ounces bittersweet chocolate, to decorate (optional)

1 Pour the cream into a saucepan. Bring to a boil over medium heat. Remove from heat and add the chocolate, all at once. Stir gently until melted. Stir in the butter until melted, then stir in the brandy. Strain into a bowl and cool to room temperature. Cover the mixture with plastic wrap and chill for 4 hours or overnight.

2 Line a large baking sheet with baking parchment. Using a small ice cream scoop, melon baller or tablespoon, scrape up the mixture into 20 large balls or 30 medium balls and place on the lined baking sheet. Dip the scoop or spoon in cold water occasionally, to prevent the mixture from sticking.

3 If dusting with cocoa powder, sift a thick layer of cocoa onto a dish or pie plate. Roll the truffles in the cocoa, rounding them between the palms of your hands. (Dust your hands with cocoa to prevent the truffles from sticking.) Do not worry if the truffles are not perfectly round. Or, roll the truffles in very finely chopped pistachios. Chill on the paper-lined baking sheet until firm. Keep refrigerated for up to 10 days or freeze for up to 2 months.

4 If coating with chocolate, do not roll the truffles in cocoa, but freeze them for 1 hour. For perfect results, temper the chocolate. Or, simply melt it in a heatproof bowl over a saucepan of barely simmering water. Using a fork, dip the truffles, one at a time, into the melted chocolate, tapping the fork on the edge of the bowl to shake off excess. Place on a baking sheet, lined with baking parchment. If the chocolate begins to thicken, reheat it gently until smooth. Chill the truffles until set.

MALT WHISKEY TRUFFLES

MAKES 25–30

*7 ounces dark chocolate, chopped into small
pieces
⅔ cup heavy cream
3 tablespoons malt whiskey
¾ cup confectioners' sugar
cocoa powder, for coating*

1 Melt the chocolate in a heatproof bowl over a saucepan of simmering water, stir until smooth, then cool slightly.

2 Using a wire whisk, whip the cream with the whiskey in a bowl until thick enough to hold its shape.

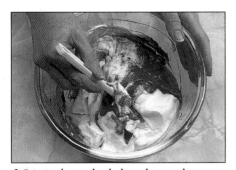

3 Stir in the melted chocolate and confectioners' sugar, mixing evenly, then let set until firm enough to handle.
4 Dust your hands with cocoa powder and shape the mixture into bite-size balls. Coat in cocoa powder and pack into paper wrappers or boxes. Store in the refrigerator for up to 3–4 days if necessary.

TRUFFLE-FILLED EASTER EGG

MAKES 1 LARGE, HOLLOW EASTER EGG

12 ounces couverture, tempered, or
unsweetened, milk or white chocolate, melted
Chocolate Truffles

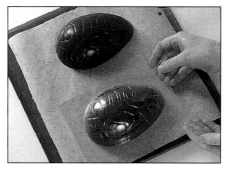

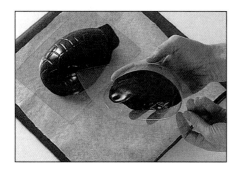

1 Line a small baking sheet with baking parchment. Using a small ladle or spoon, pour in enough melted chocolate to coat both halves of an Easter egg mold. Tilt the half-molds slowly to coat the sides completely; pour any excess chocolate back into the bowl. Set the half-molds, open side down, on the prepared baking sheet and leave for 1–2 minutes until just set.

2 Apply a second coat of chocolate and chill for 1–3 more minutes, until set. Repeat a third time, then replace the molds on the baking sheet and chill for at least 1 hour or until the chocolate has set completely. (Work quickly to avoid having to temper the chocolate again; untempered chocolate can be reheated if it hardens.)

3 To remove the set chocolate, place a half-mold, open side up, on a board. Carefully trim any drops of chocolate from the edge of the mold. Gently insert the point of a small knife between the chocolate and the mold to break the air lock. Repeat with the second mold.

4 Holding the mold open side down, squeeze firmly to release the egg half. Repeat with the other half and chill, loosely covered. (Do not touch the chocolate surface with your fingers, to avoid fingerprints.) Reserve any melted chocolate to reheat for "glue."

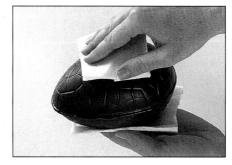

5 To assemble the egg, hold one half of the egg with a piece of paper towel or foil and fill with small truffles. If necessary, use the remaining melted chocolate as "glue." Spread a small amount onto the rim of the egg half and, holding the empty egg half with a piece of paper towel or foil, press it onto the filled half, making sure the rims are aligned and carefully attached.

6 Hold for several seconds, then prop up the egg with the paper towel or foil and chill to set. If you like, decorate the egg with ribbons or Easter decorations.

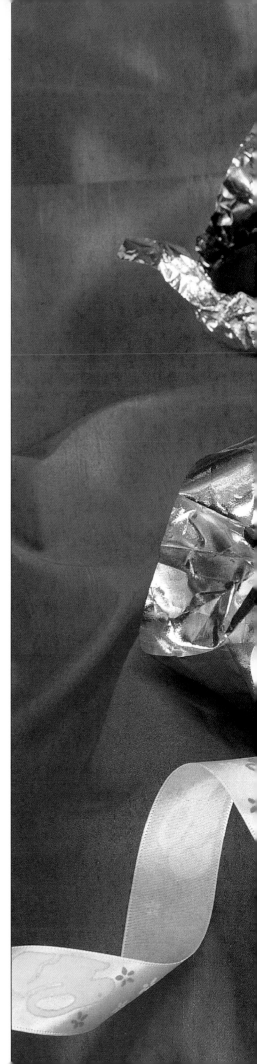

INDEX